The Price of My Dream

The Cap-it Story

**My dream, "after seducing me
with grandeur would shake me with fear"**

Hank Funk

ISBN 978-1-64114-624-1 (paperback)
ISBN 978-1-64114-625-8 (digital)

Christian Faith Publishing, Inc.
832 Park Avenue
Meadville, PA 16335
www.christianfaithpublishing.com

Printed in the United States of America

Note to the Reader

Dear Reader

Please allow me to tell my story in the fashion and artistic point of view that has become part of my personality. The philosophy and spiritual component that I speak about is a combination of values that have been my absolute strength throughout my life. The emotion that I show here has been included to help you understand the depth and gravity of what I have experienced.

DEDICATION

To my wife, Elaine, to whom I owe so much: it was my dream, not hers, but she helped me achieve it. She was the one person who stood by me as the winds of change taught us the laws on the universe. And to my two boys, Mason and Andrew; my daughters-in-law, Brenda and Kimberly who have helped to make us such a close, loving family.

If you can imagine it, you can achieve it. If you can dream it, you can become it.

—William Arthur Ward

Acknowledgements

Thanks to my many heroes, most of whom I have never met—individuals who attempted mighty things and achieved them. It was them who inspired me and gave me the strength to carry on.

Dr. Robert Schuller—Former pastor of the Hour of Power TV Ministry and founder of the Chrystal Cathedral. I admire how he overcame difficulties—the building of the Crystal Cathedral and how it almost destroyed him. He's says, "At times I wished I could be run over by a bus" while on his way to the church during its construction. The project was so massive and over budget that he thought it wouldn't be built, and saw the embarrassment that would come along with it, this while preaching a message of positive thinking and faith.

Donald Trump—I admired his confidence and how he overcame near financial destruction.

Jimmy Pattison—I admired how he conquered bankruptcy and his ordeal fighting Maple Leaf in the early days

Conrad Hilton—I admired his determination to get things he wanted.

Henry Ford—I admired his creativity and pursuit of perfection.

Norman Vincent Peale—I admired his strength and positivity, as shown in his book, *The Power of Positive Thinking.*

Al and Betty Salinger—Founders of Dufferin Games Room Stores Franchise.

Contents

Introduction

The Price of My Dream is the product of over forty years in business, twenty-seven of those years in a franchising business. Although this book is a compilation of lessons I have learned through direct experience, a great deal of what I know today was assembled from a fairly relentless pursuit of self-education, attendance at countless seminars, and reading everything I could get my hands on.

From the philosophy of Soren Kierkegaard to the entrepreneurial legend of Henry Ford, my quest for knowledge continues to this day. In this book, I will describe some of the many individuals and publications that have influenced my values and personal goals.

Much of my time was spent in search of a single book that I could identify with in terms of my struggles. I always hoped that someone understood and might possibly be able to share a philosophy that could guide me through the tough times. I found no such book. My hope is that this book, my book, will not only encourage young men and women to excel, but also comfort them in their struggles as they aspire to grow and pursue their own dreams.

What is the purpose of the book? How will it encourage people to excel? What will comfort them in their struggles? What will they learn from reading this book?

A Word About the Quotes

Whenever possible, I have noted the authors, but most are published without attribution, but with gratitude, as I have no idea where I found them. To those people I give my sincerest thanks, and if anyone can identify the sources, I will be pleased to acknowledge them.

1   My First Job

It was 1967, I was 19 years old working at Modern Building Supplies in Abbotsford. My job was truck driver, delivering building materials and lumber to construction sites. It was my first real steady job after graduating from high school and I loved it. Waking up at 6 in the morning ready for work at 7am was a little difficult. I had just graduated and entering the world of working for a living was different. However, I remember the people I worked with to be very nice. I believe the boss favored me. I guess he hadn't seen many just out of school students work at the pace as I had.

My Dad had instructed me to always show up on time and impress them with my work ethic. He wanted me to be known as a hard-working guy. One thing I did glean from my parents was how to work, show up on time and listen to the boss. As I look back upon those days now, a young man at home, the work ethic was everything. We were taught how to work. Never taught how to relax or enjoy ourselves or to enjoy a vacation. Everything was geared towards earning a living and that could only be done by working hard.

As the second youngest child in the family, nine years behind my oldest brother, I found it difficult to compete with the older three siblings. Not knowing who I was or what I was going to become and sometimes misunderstood by my parents, I became the rebel in the family. If there was something that I didn't agree with I would just go my own way.

The fact that I ran away from home three times had nothing to do with the fact that I loved my parents. I just felt I was misunderstood. My dad was 31 years older than I was and I guess he found it difficult to relate to young people and their needs. The result of running away led to self confidence.

I remember the day, it was pivotal in my determination to make a change. Even if my parents or brother and sisters believed otherwise, I was going to make something of myself. I had received much respect from the managers and workers of the company, something I hadn't found at home. I guess that is what led me to the day that something inside me transformed.

I would arrive at the lumberyard at 6:45am 15 minutes before the doors opened at 7:00am. We had to be at work before store opening, lights had to be turned on, open 4 large warehouse doors, drive the forklift into the yard, check the oil in the delivery trucks and set up the outside displays and so on. We had to be ready when doors opened and customers arrived.

It was a morning like this, I remember so well, I made the decision. It was dark and cold walking into the warehouse, trying to find the light switch. Once the light was turned on I could locate the warehouse bay door. And once the large doors were open the light from outside would stream into the warehouse. However, before we could open the doors we had to unbolt a long 12-inch-thick deadbolt that locked each side of the bay door. I found myself kicking the winged deadbolt with the toe of my boot until it would finally unwind and eventually release itself from the door frame.

This was the routine. Like everyone else I was still sluggish from the 5:30am alarm clock and still waking up. I decided that I wanted to make a difference in life, become proud of myself and I thought I'd use this little gesture as a symbol of my desire to change. This time I would go down on my knees, grab and turn the winged threaded deadbolt with my hands instead of just walking up to it and kicking it with my toe till it unwound. It was a symbol of the effort I was willing to make to change the direction in my life.

I had every reason to stay angry and become bitter from the years of my youth. Running away from home so many times gave me every excuse to be rebellious. I could have given up and become involved in alcohol or drugs like so many of the kids back then. But

I had made a decision not to follow the others. I had big dreams and a goal to achieve. It was more important to me that I buy that 1965 Mustang I had been shopping for and rent that apartment in Abbotsford's newest building.

2 Why This Dream?

For as long as I can remember, I've wanted to become a businessman. That's a challenge I've always wanted to master. Buying and selling goods, owning my own store, having employees, building beautiful and attractive displays, meeting customers, selling them my wares, and depending on myself.

Young men's dreams are as different as the young men who dream them. I was feeling stifled by my family's efforts, working toward a better life, my dreams were not for higher pay or for more responsibility over time. Rather, I pictured owning my own business, and that would make it possible for me to afford all my desires.

My dreams grew, as I did, in Abbotsford, British Columbia—where my father worked as an expert craftsman in a manufacturing facility called Dueck's Sash & Door. After some years, he opened his own millwork shop to build custom wood railings, where he worked until he retired.

As a teen, I lived for the evenings, when I could go to the basement of our house and exercise my creativity by painting, (oils or acrylics) silk-screening signs and truck lettering for some of the local businesses: real estate companies, trucking companies, and retailers. I didn't want to be like my dad, as I perceived him—lonely, with no hobby but work, and so devoted to working hard that he got sick, and without much monetary reward. Even though he never spent more than he made, he never took risks; he was a cautious and thrifty man who took care of his family. His approach to life just didn't appeal to me.

***

I was seventeen years old and had already started to think increasingly about business ideas. I do remember a time even earlier, when I was five years old my neighborhood friend and I were trying to sell painted clay objects of some kind that we hand-made set up in a roadside stand. Of course, nobody even stopped to look, but we had fun building our colored assortment of stuff and pretending. I was a retailer even at that age.

I had graduated and found myself curious about the silk-screening process. I happened to see it in action one day and was amazed by how it worked. I could print anything I wanted and as many copies as needed. I drove to Vancouver, an hour out of town, to buy a small demo kit. I carefully read the instructions, and then I began to silk-screen print.

The following week, I asked a local real estate company in town if they needed new real estate signs, told them I was the guy that did silk screening. Don't really remember how I did it, but I got the order after giving him a quote for 100 double-faced plywood real estate For Sale signs. It must have been the beautiful drawing I gave them, a new upscale design that they liked. All I remember is that I used that little demo kit I had bought and made more money than I ever thought I would. Dad let me take over the basement to silk screen the signs. Wow! They weren't expecting the whole house to smell like a paint factory.

From then on, I was in business. I was unafraid, not knowing what I was capable of. All I knew was that I had a sales pitch, and I could get the order. The following year, I painted hundreds of No Parking signs for the Abbotsford International Airshow, which happened to become a repeat customer. I had no overhead; I was using my dad's basement and so I could out-bid anyone. From there, business just increased.

I also trained myself to use the Fitch sign lettering brushes along with the specialized One Shot paint, and lettered many trucks, buses, and airplanes through the years. There were no computers that cut vinyl letters; lettering was all done by the skill of the hand. This small business gave me plenty of cash while I was living with my parents. I was never out of money.

I called my business Hank's Signs. The sign business continued for many years after I married and got a job in 1970 giving me extra income working evenings and weekends.

I was so young! I had graduated from high school, and shortly afterward got married, and found myself working at Modern Building Supplies. I knew there had to be a better way for me. I wanted my life to be easier, and more fun. I knew a large part of my dream was unfulfilled, and after a few years of working there, I knew it was time for a change.

It was at that time that a couple of local business acquaintances thought that collaborating with me to buy even bigger silk-screening equipment would be an excellent idea. By then, I had already had a contract to paint the City of Abbotsford's traffic signs after hours. I rented an old empty house and did the painting there because the apartment we lived in was too small. The plan was to silk-screen traffic signs for many cities across the province. Art had always been my first love, and I enjoyed the way these guys were talking. I entered into a business partnership with the two brothers. And without a partnership agreement, we carried on. I left my good-paying job at Modern Lumber in Abbotsford and moved to their acreage, where we set up our business and shop in their large back building. We called ourselves BC's Signs & Silk Screening Ltd. A few years later, we renamed it Continental Traffic Signs, and then were finally bought out by a company in Surrey called Astrographics. It's still in business today.

***

I took on partners without a business plan or doing due diligence. They were professional business men with good work ethics. I was just too young and thought everyone had the same goals as I had or placed the same values on the company's priorities. The partners meant well but in the end, we had to go our own way.

While trying to marshal my thoughts into a workable plan, my family encouraged me to abandon my own business and take a salaried position at another lumberyard, Dueck Building Supplies. After all, I was young; I had my whole life ahead of me and would lose only five thousand dollars that I had invested in that business. My dad had cosigned for that amount but couldn't know that it would take me four long and difficult years to pay it back.

I did accept a position at Dueck's. At first, I sold lumber supplies; and afterward, I traveled from store to store, setting up displays and giving the old lumberyard a badly needed improved look. I was a store decorator while being a salesman. In my fourth year at Dueck's, I was asked to join the carpet sales division, where a manager would prophesy that I might want to try running my own show. He would never know the fire his words lit in me.

I loved to watch him work, and I knew that my youthful enthusiasm would thrive on the very pressures he experienced. Working as his employee was great. I didn't have to live through those long, late evenings being self-employed, while my lonely wife sat at home, waiting for me. I would never have cash flow problems, nor would I have those excruciatingly intense discussions with my partners.

I was at peace—at least for a little while. My talent for sales began to pay off; I was bringing in six to ten times more money a month, on commission, selling more carpets than the average employee. But it wouldn't last.

I developed a strategy for selling carpet to high-rise buildings and making lots of money, both for myself and the company. Firstly, I'd get the contract for the entire high-rise tower by outbidding the competitor. I would price it out at a very low margin of 15%. That was low in that period of time. However, it was conditional that the developers allow me a display suite on the first or second floor, for easy access. The display suite had the specified carpet installed; however, the catch was that they would allow me to up-sell the new suite owners as they walked in. The display suite looked like a retail carpet showroom. I would get nine out of ten people to upgrade to the better-quality carpet and tile. The margins now jumped to 40%. Was my boss happy? Everyone was happy—the customer, myself, and the company.

Three years after my promising start, the economy slowed, and people stopped buying new homes. It was the early 1970s, and the company's demand that I replace those lost sales eventually led to my leaving Dueck's.

One day, while trying to get my camper electrically wired to my truck, I happened to meet Albert Nickel, the owner of Rover Industries. I saw that he had built his little company all by himself, selling truck canopies, campers, and RV supplies. A survey of his store showed me that it was messy and disorganized. Customers had to step over products lying on the floor. There were no displays or organized shelving.

Here was a chance for a young man like me to test my mettle. I came out of the store and talked with Albert—a tall, intense, eccentric man, whom I respected for his approach to business—and asked him if he would like to hire a first-rate salesperson like me.

"Yes, but I can't pay you much," he replied.

I shot back, "You don't need to. I'll earn my way." And I began my career at Rover Industries. Changing from a white-shirt-and-tie-guy to a casual dressed jean wearing salesman, I assumed my new position.

It gave me great satisfaction to help improve his store and his bottom line. Just watching him perform in his own peculiar way gave me a better understanding of the basics of running a small business. Cash-ups and banking, ordering products, receiving shipments, and making money on everything he did or sold—all these activities filled my mind with the things I would someday need. Suddenly, it was five years later, and I felt it was time to move on. But where?

I sensed that the *where* would really determine *what* my dream was. I've always believed that every legitimate desire creates a magnetic force, attracting the fulfillment of that need, if you will put every effort of energy and faith into it. At night, while drifting off to sleep, I envisioned owning my own store. But to choose and reach my destination, I would need some luck. Luck reared its head just weeks later. Albert had shared with me the struggles and pains of growing his small company.

Rover's manufacturing division made the truck canopies and sold them to Rover's retail store. Sales had increased, but so had the difficult task of hiring staff. With a determined face, Albert held up his hands as if to ask for my help.

"Might you be interested in purchasing one division?" he said.

Without thinking, I said, "Yes, I would be interested." My next thought was where could the money come from? I agreed to take the division he wanted the least. I bought the retail truck canopy (store) division. He wanted to keep the manufacturing division. It didn't matter to me. I would finally have my own business.

Working in carpet sales had afforded my wife and me the luxury of acquiring a five-acre hobby farm in Aldergrove, and it would be this property that would offer us the opportunity to increase the mortgage in order to finance the purchase of one of Albert's divisions. Suddenly, I was in business.

I was speechless, overcome with joy beyond my wildest dreams. I remember selling my first truck (Cap) canopy. While installing it, the thought came to me, *I can keep all the gross profit.* It was *mine,* not the boss's! And I would do the very best I could with it from now on.

3 Early Adventures in Business

October 7, 1977, was the day I took over Rover Industries Ltd. and I ran it successfully for thirteen years. Rover had begun by selling truck canopies, truck caps, the shells that you install to enclose the bed of a pickup truck. The truck cap goes under several other names, each depending on what part of the country you are from. In BC, we called it a truck canopy; in the USA, it can be called a camper shell. Our industry, the Light Truck Accessory Association, (LTAA), is trying to get everyone to call it the Truck Cap.

Our two boys, Mason and Andrew, were five and three years old; and I was twenty-nine, full of all the necessary energy and perseverance required to run the business successfully. My wife, Elaine, would do the bookkeeping and take care of the boys. We changed the company name to Rover Recreation Centre, because of all the diversity in products we were selling.

It was the spring of 1978. The store was busy, and good help was hard to find. We placed another help wanted ad in the local paper. In those days, businesses would get the word out by placing an ad in the local newspaper, under the classifieds, in the help wanted section. There was no Craigslist or internet forum.

I had always wanted my brother to come in with me as partner in the early years but he had a successful career teaching in Winnipeg as professor of architecture. I know that it was my dads' dream to have both of his sons involved with him in business, but times never allowed for that. Dad was just so happy in the early 1960's to finally have a steady paying job. And probably didn't realize that risk-taking was not in his nature. So, both sons went their own way. Dad stayed at his job for 17 years and brother Harold, still in Winnipeg manages his own architectural firm. As for me, as the second and youngest of his sons, I didn't mind taking risks. I knew I could make it work even if I did it alone.

Despite my continual search for a good employee to help the small and growing company, no one answered the ad. At least no one that I would consider hiring. Months had passed with little results. One day a friend of mine suggested that his new immigrant brother-in-law might fit the bill. Sales were great that spring and so out of desperation I agreed, even if it meant the brother-in-law would just help keep the place clean, neat and tidy and so I agreed. However, we would keep searching for the right person to fill the position.

I remember his first day on the job, I quite enjoyed observing him. The speed at which he moved was refreshing. The British accent together with the way he carried himself, polite, well spoken and always willing to please made an impression. He had worked for a large company in London for 25 years and brought with him an interesting resume. I still remember the one comment on the resume, "Alan was always willing to attend to any distress that might occur in a distant outpost". I could tell from this that he must have been a loyal and dedicated employee. I like loyalty above all, it has always been a trait I have looked for when interviewing applicants.

It appears that currently young people feel they need to have a lot of work experience and to them that means changing jobs every year or two. Sticking with a growing company and making a career out if it is not common place anymore. However, I knew I needed some loyal, reliable staff as I built the company.

Alan worked hard each day, now working in the service shop installing truck canopies and fitting them to the bed of pick-up trucks. "Wow can this guy move" I said, he would actually jump in and out of the back of the pick-up truck bed and run to the bench to get more tools for the job. I hadn't seen this kind of effort for a long while. Alan stayed with the company and continued to apply himself in his strange unfamiliar country. "You don't see these kinds of pick-up trucks in London", Alan would say. "Just reverse your lorry to the back and I'll put it in the boot" meant, back up your truck and I'll put it in the trunk.

A little while later, as luck would have it, a nice well-dressed lady walked into our store and asked for a job. She would not take no for an answer. Her work experience was in groceries as a cashier and in bookkeeping. Exuded with confidence she continued to impress me with her energy. She had no knowledge or experience in the truck accessory world and I felt that the change might be too difficult for her. Energy is another attribute that I have always looked for in people. I hired her for that reason alone.

When I look back on these two individuals I must say, I will never forget the important role they played in the success of growing our company. Ceka became manager of the RV, camping and billiard departments. She was great with customers, they loved her even when she would discipline them or embarrassed them. I remember one day a middle-aged man came in smoking a cigarette. Remember in the seventies many people smoked while walking into a retail store. That was normal for that time. I even remember Alan, the polite sales person, would always place his lit cigarette under the sales counter before he addressed the customer. The ashtray on the sales counter was reserved for customers only, in his mind.

This middle-aged man walks into the store and butted his cigarette on the showroom vinyl tiled floor stepping on it with the toe of his boot. Ceka had just cleaned the floor that morning. Well Ceka didn't hold back, looking straight at the customer she asked, "do you butt your cigarette on your wife's floor at home, do yah?", she belted out. Customer looked at her rather stunned. "Then why do you do it on my floor?" she continued. Strange thing is the customer picked it up off the floor with a smirk and continued to buy the item he was looking at. She always managed get away with things like this, where if we had tried, a fight might have broken out. It must have been the twinkle in her eye and her sneaky smile that gave customers the feeling she was their sister. I remember another time when a customer was haggling over a price. In his mind, it was priced too high, but her comment to him was, "you probably don't even have that much money in your wallet". And to prove her wrong, he paid the full price with a laugh and a smile. She was a pleasure to work with and joy to have in the company. Ceka, Alan, and myself were an invincible trio for many years.

Ceka worked in sales, bookkeeping and in purchasing. If you were a Vendor, look out, she would get the best price from anyone.

Alan was like a magician in my mind. No one could "pull a rabbit out of a hat" like Alan. Many times I found myself going to Alan a few days before month-end and tell him we needed to bring in another $20K before month end closes, and he would make it happen. Time after time he would help us achieve our sales budget. His favorite line to customers was, "leave it to me, I'll take care of it for you" and he did. However, there were a few cases where I had to step in and help him out.

Alan hated paper-work but his success in sales would always be cause for forgiveness. It is a common thing in many businesses, as it was in ours, that sales covers sins. The trail of mistakes and paper-work errors would always be forgotten when I saw the high amount of sales he had closed and finalized.

Alan Sealey worked for us for 30 years. A man that I dearly love for what he helped us achieve. He was always willing to help me out in times of trouble. Even after he retired he would come back in, fly out to another province to help a failing store to boost their lagging sales. I remember saying to those franchisee who needed help and wanted to learn how to sell or teach their staff to sell, "when Alan walks into your store watch and see how he does it, your sales will go up immediately". And quite often he would close a canopy sale or two with in the first day. He just had a knack for getting the customers trust and closing the sale, even if he got the customers' last $10 in their wallet as a deposit. Customers loved him.

I spent most of my life in retail sales and I can tell you customers like to be sold. In training, I always teach my students to remember to ask questions without the customer ever recognizing it. Listen more than you speak and remember to ask for the order. I can confidently say that Alan's closing rate would have been a minimum 8 out of 10 for every customer that phoned or walked in the store.

The odd time I will hear someone in the organization say that they want to be an Alan, too - a "keeper". They are referring to someone that stays with the company and makes it a life career.

Henry Matties was another person in our town that had tremendous effect on my early success. The rumour in town was that he was a difficult man to do business with. I found the opposite. Matties became our landlord and I must say, one of the best landlords we have ever had. I found him to be honest, fair, and always looking out for the other guy. He was a very successful businessman. He owned and operated the biggest independent furniture store in town and was a builder of many apartment blocks and commercial properties in the community.

He saw how I had improved the fledgling truck canopy store and wanted to help it grow. We had just moved to the new location on South Fraser Way at the west end of town. Matties had convinced us to move into his new 7,000 sq. foot commercial building. We signed a three-year lease and it was shortly after that when he introduced me to the Sundance Trampoline manufacturer in Vancouver. He had been selling trampolines on the side at his house while running his furniture store and felt it would be a better fit in our business. He asked if I wanted the dealership, all I had to do was buy his existing inventory of $10K. He wanted me to carry on and give the trampolines a home.

The decision to take on the Sundance dealership was a lot of money for me at that time, but it was a good choice. It lead us to the ever so popular Rebounder, the mini trampoline, also manufactured by Sundance. Books were being published at the time about the many benefits of the Rebounder. Studies described and documented proof that regular rebounding could reduce your body fat, firm your arms, benefit the shape of your legs, hips and abdomen, improve your balance, stimulate your lymphatic system, protect your joints, strengthen your muscles and bones ... and so on.

Rebounders were selling for $249.00 throughout the country in 1978. When we brought it in to our store, Sundance was just beginning to manufacture the identical item at a lower cost so we could retail it at $199.00. We had no idea what to expect or the kind of response we would receive. Especially after we put it on sale one weekend for $159.00. After our first newspaper ad, we had customers lining up outside the door before the store opened. WOW, that was a retailer's dream. I don't ever remember another item that ever created such a buzz like the Rebounder. It was not unusual for us to sell 100 in a week.

The reason for the hype was that the originators of the Rebounder chose to market the mini-trampoline years earlier across North America through a home sales commission party process. Individuals would set up parties and promote the book of Rebounding to sell the mini- trampoline. This was a perfect set up for us, the many years of door to door marketing had created a demand for the product. Customers were now educated in the product and all we had to do was lower the price.

The following year, Matties sold his furniture store so he could spend more time building apartment complexes and developing commercial properties. The new owners didn't want the National billiard tables he had on display at the furniture store. So again, he asked if I would like to become a dealer with National billiards and take over for him. I said yes, and the rest is history. Billiard tables were another huge success for us.

There were many things that catapulted us to a higher level of success in those early years. First, it was the large building we leased from Matties. It was much larger than we required, but strangely enough, it worked well as we continued to expand. Secondly, the Sundance Trampoline business together with the National Billiard Table dealership gave us the additional profits we needed. When we add in the great staff and especially the two key managers, Ceka & Alan, we had a store that was firing on all cylinders. We had a smooth, successful and profitable running business.

When I look back even through all the difficulties, I can see that I have had a lot of good luck along the way. I have not forgotten the people who helped me. I recall thanking Matties for all his help and mentorship before he passed away at the age of 81 in 2010. He was an entrepreneur extraordinaire, an individual that not only knew how to do business well, improve the community, but how to recognize others who would accept his help and take his advice.

Business Coach

In 1981 I had a visitor that walked in our store named, Terry Garner, the host of the TV show, Reach for The Top. Reach for The Top was a popular TV show in Canada at the time, an educational quiz show, where a panel of students competed with other schools in a quiz of knowledge. Garner was hired by the Federal Business Development Bank of Canada (FBDB) now known as BDC (Business Development Bank of Canada) to produce a documentary on how FBDB not only loaned money to small businesses, but helped them in business through their coaching method. Something other Canadian banks had not thought of.

I was extremely excited. Rover had been chosen out of three other businesses in British Columbia to be in this documentary. It must have been my passion for business during the interview that made Garner choose me over the others. It was FBDB that financed the purchase of Rover Recreation several years earlier and somehow we got on their list. We were told that they planned to do a 30-minute documentary that would be shown across English speaking Canada.

FBDB had assigned a business coach to me. His name was Gerry Culver. He graduated from university at an early age, earning the Lieutenant Governor's award. Gerry joined the Hudson's Bay Company at 16 as a stock boy in the Vancouver store. He retired 44 years later as the manager of the Richmond Bay. He then joined FBDB and began his second career as a CASE counsellor travelling throughout BC consulting with small businesses. He continued this into his 80's because he loved helping people and was having so much fun.

When I heard that someone of this stature was to be my business coach I was overwhelmed. It was a dream of mine, to have someone help me, especially with all the questions I had about business. I was 33 years old and eager to learn.

I remember one of the first visits we had, I was not impressed, somewhat disappointed. He kept asking me about the burned out light bulb in the showroom and why it still hadn't been replaced and why the carpet by the coke machine was dirty. He pointed out the tidiness of the showroom. I thought he was nuts, who does he think he is? Finally, after the second visit he spoke about the training he received working at the Bay. Their number one goal was cleanliness, customer care and then profits. I thought it was just the opposite. I wanted to know how to make money first and then I'd clean up the store.

He taught me that every detail was important in business. I guess that is why I keep preaching this message still today to our franchisees, "To succeed you have to get as many things right as possible" something few people understand.

He pointed out the basic rules of retailing. As an example, he taught me an empty pegboard hook is a lost sale. And that each item needs to have a price ticket on it, not beside it or close to it, but on the actual item. And that customers in general don't have the time to search for the price, it should be at eye level, easy to notice. He says, think of a child and what it takes to get their attention. Same goes for the adult customer. Make it easy for customers to shop.

I wanted him to give me shortcuts on how I could make more money and improve the store. But in return he pointed out the simplest methods of being a very successful retailer and how to out perform the competitor. Hudson's Bay was probably the most successful department store of its time in the 1960's–1970's and are still in business today. Here was a man that had proven himself, managing the biggest department store in BC store, doing millions of dollars in sales and I had the gall to critique his efforts.

I can identify with our franchisees and their reluctance to listen. I know what they are thinking when we come to visit their store. I was the same. Franchisees in general think the ingredients to running a successful store is complicated. However, the **system** is easy, so easy they can be reluctant to follow it. Our motto; *follow the **system** and you are going to make money, ignore the **system** and you will pay a price.* I learned this from the best and it has given me much success.

The Garner production team, guest actors and coaches filled the store with excitement. Cameras were set up and the shooting began. The filming took about a week to complete. I still have the video. It was a great time which also helped point me in the direction of coaching others and ultimately led to us franchising our concept.

Culver told me I had a talent for selecting good products, merchandizing and marketing. I just needed to take care of the smallest details and understand the basics of retailing and finance. Like watching the monthly (P&L's) monthly profit and loss statements. He was always impressed with our fine-looking displays and the excitement it created for the customer. I had learned valuable lessons from Culver, it was just what I needed to fuel my desire to build the store even bigger and better.

Little by little, we increased the product mix: canoes, RV supplies, truck accessories, National billiard tables, swimming pool supplies, Beachcomber hot tubs, patio furniture, Sundance trampolines, and, finally, the Eagle Ultralight airplane. It was an assortment of things that we felt added up to great fun. We truly intended to live up to the name *Recreation Centre*. It was a very successful time for us. Many customers commented that they had never seen a store as exciting as ours.

4 How Our Company Evolved

It was a special time for business, for consumers, and for the government. Retailers were enjoying great sales; consumer confidence was at its highest. Homeowners began to realize their home values had increased, giving them greater equity. Our national debt was reduced because of inflation; however, the Feds knew that inflation had to be stopped and controlled, or there would be serious trouble. Our government has been very carefully watching the inflation rate since that time. They never want to see it spiral out of control like it did in the late seventies and early eighties. It was 1981 when bank home mortgage interest rates reached the very high level of 19%. Can you imagine your monthly mortgage payment all of a sudden doubling? Many people lost their homes because they couldn't make their monthly payment.

Business was booming because of the high interest rate, but the word on the street was *Might as well buy now before your money becomes worthless.* Commercial property was almost doubling in value in a matter of months. Land was selling so fast that there wasn't enough commercially zoned land to go around, and the shortage created an even higher demand. Land and consumer goods cost got higher and higher each day. Nobody knew when it would end, so people kept buying. Lots of money was made in buying and selling.

Some people got caught speculating during this time. Several friends of mine got caught up in buying land, for example, at $250,000 and selling it a month or two later for $400,000.

I can remember the day when everything came to a standstill. Those people who had bought land for $400,000 suddenly couldn't get their money back. There were no buyers. Everyone wanted to see where the roller coaster would bottom out before they purchased again. It would take many years before land regained its prior value. During this time, individuals who had leveraged their purchases would be making large payments on property that was now worth less than they had paid. Many people went broke.

Guys like me never forgot the lessons we learned and how people with great ideals might suffer. Anyone who went through that period of time in business will never forget the value of not overextending yourself or taking risks on borrowed money.

For retailers like us, it wasn't so bad. We made lots of money. We didn't take losses like the land speculators, but we did feel the effects of the crash. As an example, in an average month, our store would generate approximately $100,000 in revenue. The day after the crash, our sales never went above $50,000. Revenues had dropped by 50%. We just had to get used to it. The economic changes were dramatic. Retailers scrambled to adapt.

After the crash, London Drugs, a chain of stores in Canada, became popular in the early seventies by selling at discount pricing. London Drugs became one of our biggest competitors. Now they were selling pool chemicals and patio furniture at our cost. Then, what appeared to come out of nowhere was a huge warehouse-style concept called Price Club, now known as Costco. They became famous for selling everything from groceries to watches at steep discount prices.

One of our most profitable items was the Sundance trampoline. Costco was now selling a similar round trampoline for half the price of the Sundance. All this change took place in a matter of twelve months. We were the largest Sundance Trampoline dealer in Canada, and ours retailed for $1,599. We had no problems selling the trampoline at that price until Costco brought out their round trampoline for $699. A few years later, they would sell that same trampoline for only $399.

We knew that the world had changed and we'd have to do something about it. I had heard a Canadian statistic that said 95%

of all businesses go broke in five years, and 95% have less than 50 employees. The odds of an independent business like ours staying in business were slim. However, for us, failure was never an option. We would have to find a solution to the problem.

During these years, I envied London Drugs and their ability to buy so well because they were connected to the right people and suppliers. The idea of franchising slowly grew in my mind. I wanted to be a part of a system and a team that could take us through tough years like these, and give us the ability to compete, no matter which competitors we had.

It was all about money and who could sell products at the lowest price. We now had extremely price-conscious consumers. The big-box stores like the Home Depot and Costco became very popular. Small ma-and-pa businesses had to shut down. Small local hardware stores came to an end just like small local stationery stores ended because of Staples, Office Depot, and Home Depot.

The same thing happened in the furniture business. The big department stores of old could not react fast enough to the now-price-conscious consumer. After the recession, the retail landscape had changed completely. Those that could adapt survived. And those that couldn't went out of business. United Buy & Sell, or what today is called United Furniture Warehouse, became popular (189 stores in 2001). The Rock Furniture, Harry Hammer, and the Brick grew and opened stores (235) in many locations. These new companies had solved the supply problem and offered furniture for very low price—something that Sears and the Hudson Bay could not do at the time.

I admire the French; they did not permit the large American bread manufacturers to set up their factories in France. They didn't want large factories to destroy their small ma-and-pa bakeries. If you travel to Paris, all you'll see there are thousands of small bread bakery shops serving the people.

How Retailing Changed

The business triangle

best price

best service

best inventory

The new business triangle law said if your company is offering all three—best price, best service, and best inventory—then your company won't be self-sustaining; and chances are that you will go broke. A store must choose two out of the three just to survive. Providing all three services is cost-prohibitive. The missing item must be camouflaged or cloaked; customers believe that you are offering all three, when in fact, you cannot. Some hide the lack of the best service with a money-back guarantee. They have neither the money nor the time, to spend with you to ensure that this item is the right one for you. Instead, they will permit you to waste your time in returning the item.

Big-box stores usually offer the best inventory and the best price, but seldom the best service. Specialty stores can offer the best service and the best inventory but seldom the best price.

Recessions bring about a totally new way of doing business. I call it "adapt or get out of the way." So it was with us. These years taught us the value of being connected to a buying group, a system, and a strategy.

Stores like Bed Bath & Beyond operate on another strategy in retailing, and they make no bones about it. A close friend of mine worked there and was told by the manager while in training, "Listen, people. We sell things that customers really don't need, so let's make the items look as good as possible: fill the shelves deep, wide, and high. Let's give them a total-satisfaction guarantee. Let's give them service that is better than any competitor's." The store may sell things people might not need, but the enticement is so high, prices are so low, and the variety is so great you can hardly help yourself. They offer products at such low prices customers tell themselves, *I've never seen such great variety and selection at such low pricing that I have to buy it.* The funny thing is, in the end, most of it ends up in someone's garage sale—but you had fun buying it. Again, we are in a consumer price-conscious age, and we love to buy.

To survive, we had to dismantle Rover Recreation and divide it into three stores: a swimming pool store, a billiard table store, and a truck canopy store. Each store specialized with its own product, with the best price and the best service. Had we not made these changes, we would have been forced out of business.

In an effort to compete on price, we found a way to buy pool chemicals directly from an Australian manufacturer called Great Lakes Pool Chemicals. It worked for us; however, we knew it wasn't the end of the efficiencies we had to institute, and we had to do more; so I took a direction from the Australian chemical company's retail division and opened a new stand-alone store under the name of Poolmart.

Even our RV supplies could be purchased for less from the neighboring RV lot, Fraserway Campers. They too had recognized where the market was going, and because they also manufactured campers and trailers, they were actually buying directly from the manufacturer and could sell their RV supplies for less. We had to get out of the RV parts business.

Poolmart

Poolmart was a great new name. It was modern and symbolized our new approach, a specialized concept, and it worked. It was just right for the time. We specialized in the best pricing with the best service, and our customers loved it.

I enrolled three of my staff and myself in a night-school course in pool water chemistry at the British Columbia Institute of Technology

(BCIT), and we all got our commercial water chemistry certificate. We were the first store in Abbotsford to introduce an onsite/in-store pool water analysis. We called it Pool Water Doctor. We had a chemical laboratory on site, so we could test and report the customer's pool water chemistry with precision. It was an awesome time. We purchased our chemical direct from the manufacturer, unlike in the previous years.

We sold swimming pool chemicals and supplies, patio furniture, hot tubs, and Jacuzzi spas. At the time, I was experimenting whether or not to franchise this concept. I gave it a catchy name, the footprint was just the right size, capable of being placed in any strip mall, and it specialized in one thing—swimming pool equipment and supplies. The store was an instant success, which drew attention from the competition. The problem was that I had much larger dreams. All I knew was that people from all over came to see what they thought was the beginning of a new franchise concept. Of course, some manufactures felt that if we opened more stores like this one, we were going to be a threat. Especially the Beachcomber people. Beachcomber was owned by an old friend of mine, Keith Scott of Surrey, who operated many of these stores throughout the country. Keith also owned the largest swimming pool distribution warehouses and a spa manufacturing facilities in Canada.

Dufferin Games Room

During this time, we heard that Sears had an eight-foot pool table for sale. Again, someone was selling a similar product to ours, but at much the same price as our cost. In 1984, we heard of a company in Ontario that was planning on franchising their new billiard table concept. They had taken the billiard table business and combined it with table games and called it the Dufferin Games Room.

I had what I thought was a brilliant idea. My strategy was simple. My wife and I flew to Ontario and met with Dufferin. They showed me around the facilities, their manufacturing plant, and then, finally, their new concept store in the Square One Shopping Centre in Toronto. Show a guy like me an upscale billiard table store so high-tech, something the world had never seen, and I was sold. I have never been so impressed as I was that day.

But they were hesitant to sell the franchise. They said they were not quite ready for franchising. It didn't matter to me; I took out my checkbook, wrote down a big number, and slid it over to the director of franchise development, Larry Saboriack. He reluctantly accepted it. I told him I was going to do it and I wanted him to make it happen, and purchased a Dufferin Games Room franchise, becoming their first franchisee in Canada. I also told him I would be his best franchisee, and I was. Dufferin made tables that looked much like grand pianos, either shiny black laminate finishes with red cloth, or pure white shiny laminate with red cloth. They had other color schemes no one had ever seen. Customers loved them.

Our strategy was simple. We gave the customer more variety. If Sears had one table, we had ten tables; but we had one at their price, and nine others that they didn't sell, at higher prices. A customer walking into one of our stores at the time was overwhelmed. They had never seen that much variety in our town before. We ended up being Dufferin's largest account in Canada. We inventoried hundreds of slate billiard tables, even to the point where we had to rent additional space to house the inventory. I can remember one day when we sold nine billiard tables at an average of $1,800 per table. Remember, in the early '80s, the average wage for a salesperson was $1,650 per month. We brought in professional pool players, including the British Columbian and Canadian billiard table champions, to play in our store in front of our customers on Saturday mornings. Times were good, and we made money.

By this time, retailers like ourselves very seldom bought from Brunswick Billiards. The Brunswick Corporation had many other divisions besides Bowling and Billiards. They had Life Fitness, the Brunswick Boat Group and Mercury Marine. The old billiard company of 170 years had a new competitor that paid attention to billiard table appearance, price and service. I guess they hadn't kept up with the changing times and gave way to the new up-and-coming Dufferin Games Room stores. Dufferin also carried bar accessories such as drinking glasses, dart boards, shuffle boards, decorative signs, brass bar table piping, card tables and chairs, and brass wine racks. Just about anything that you would want to have for your games room.

Our years as a Dufferin franchisee taught us the value of a franchise system. "Follow the system" was the buzz phrase. We were careful to obey and follow the system, and it worked. We made money. Al and Betty Salinger were the founders and owners of Dufferin. They became our mentors. They were polite and focused people with the same values as Elaine and I had. They were very concerned about each franchisee. I remember telling them that I wanted to be their best franchisee; I wanted to take what they had built and become part of their team. I wanted them to be proud of what I would do in British Columbia for the franchise.

Years later, Dufferin had built up their franchise to about 34 stores across Canada. They were in many malls. When Al and Betty passed away, the business went to their sons, who carried on for a while, and then ended up dissolving the company. What a sad story. Why did such a great concept fail?

I had a difficult time trying to find out what went wrong after Al and Betty passed away. The best I could tell from the conversations of current store owners, still trading under the now-defunct name *Dufferin*, was that the boys overspent and never reacted to the marketplace changes through the years, so they shut it down.

I still see the Dufferin name in billiard stores but I understand the franchise no longer exists, and the name is being used by others. My thoughts were that there's no excuse for a good company like theirs to go out of business. They manufactured billiard tables and some of the finest billiard cues in the world. They needed a reliable source to manufacture those magnificent cues. They owned land in Africa where trees for the specialized cue timbers grew. I still own one of their most expensive cues—it's made from a wood that is now banned from use—Mun Ebony and Gaboon Ebony are listed as critically endangered woods; they are at an extremely high risk of extinction in the wild in the immediate future. They are banned from crossing international borders.

Of course, this was lesson number 1: too much variety left us vulnerable in the marketplace. We thought that if we couldn't make it with the products we had, we should keep adding more and more. After the first ten years, we found that we had to split departments and create individual stores. We had created Poolmart, the Dufferin Game Store, and Rover Truck Canopies.

To a real estate salesman, I expressed my hopes that we could divest ourselves of the Dufferin and Poolmart divisions. My presentation must have convinced him that he too wanted to enjoy what I had, so he bought them both.

Can I sell or what?

Rover Truck Canopies

Now, with only one store to take care of, Elaine and I decided to take our business more seriously with the hope that our competitors might not.

The truck canopy business was a different animal. We were buying directly from the manufacturer, and so we were able to remain competitive. An opportunity came to us one day to manufacture our own aluminum truck caps (or canopies). A friend, Lyle McDowell, asked if I wanted to buy his small aluminum truck cap assembly business in Summerland, BC, and I said yes. We moved the business to Abbotsford and began manufacturing truck caps. We now had the ability to sell wholesale to other truck cap dealers and retail ourselves at the same time. No one else could touch us. Our pricing was the best.

One of our men could build five canopies per day. My labor cost to build one unit was $22. We purchased the aluminum canopies in kit form from Elkhart, Indiana, by the truckload of 200 units. We branded the canopies Toplight.

The truck cap business began to grow rapidly when the aluminum cap was introduced. It sold for only $399 in 1978. Guys in pickup trucks could now cover their truck bed in a matter of minutes, clamp it down, and drive off. It wasn't uncommon to sell as many as six to ten caps a day. However, it didn't take long before everyone wanted to get into the aluminum canopy business, so we started to sell more fiberglass truck caps. They looked better, cost more, and they could be custom-painted to match the customer's truck. Fiberglass was smooth and looked like it came directly from the truck manufacturer.

I wanted to break away from the competitive truck canopy business. Approximately four major manufacturers were located in Summerland, BC; and they were constantly trying to steal one another's customers and business. The only way out that we could see was to buy from an American manufacturer and become their exclusive dealer in Canada. Even then, with the Canadian dollar fluctuating, there were problems competing with the other Canadians.

The idea of manufacturing our own canopy came up one day when I heard of someone who could help us get into the business. He was an American, the man who invented the double-platinum vacuum-forming machine. He had already made this machine for the very successful USA cap manufacturer named Brahma. At this time it was a space-age process.

I was at a fork in the road: buying the machine would cost us $250,000 in 1980—a small fortune back then. Our studies showed that we didn't have the population to support a machine like this unless we planned to distribute into the United States as well. The question we asked ourselves at the time was *Do you want to be a manufacturer or a retailer?* If we went down the road of building or buying a vacuum-forming machine, it meant all our attention would be on manufacturing and finding distributors/retailers to sell our product.

Where would we have the most power and influence? I remember debating this with my friends at the time, and I made the decision to go the retail route. We thought many retail stores could control the manufacturing, whereas the manufacturer is totally dependent on his product and the retailer selling his product.

Our decision was correct for two reasons. First, the vacuum-forming business in the USA came to a complete stop a few years later because Dow Corning and DuPont began manufacturing inferior plastic sheets, sheets that broke or shattered in -20 degree Celcius weather. Not a good material for a truck cap in Alberta.

Second, opening a chain of stores ended up being a good choice. We could have more control of our destiny. We ended up buying our truck caps from the American manufacturer, Leer, now known as TAG (the Truck Accessory Group). Cap-it is one TAG's largest customers and therefore gets preferred service.

I found that managing three such different businesses again was too difficult, so we made plans to sell everything except the truck accessory store, and also to divest ourselves of the Eagle Ultralight division (more about Eagle in the next chapter).

5 The Eagle Flies
(A Small Diversion)

I wanted to start up another business—a business selling Ultralight Aircraft.

One of my ambitions was to fly and taste the freedom of the skies. It was the most exhilarating experience I could have wished for. I had spent much of my youth jumping off buildings in an effort to be like Superman. Would I ever get the chance to fly?

My boyhood fantasies continued until the day in 1980 when I drove by a little country field in Surrey, BC. Perseverance and determination through the years must have led me to that day. I had seen ultralight planes on TV, but never up close like this. Only fifty feet from my car, I saw the most beautiful thing in the world taxiing toward me at the roadside. It was a small kite-like airframe that resembled a miniature aircraft. The pilot came within yards of where I was parked; only the fence and the shoulder of the road kept us apart. Then without warning, he turned back in the direction he had come from, powered up, and sped down the makeshift runway. Somewhat in disbelief, I watched the tiny airframe lift the pilot ever-so-slowly toward the sky. My childhood dream had come true; someone had invented what I had only dreamed about—a slow-flying aircraft.

So the question was, how can I buy an ultralight plane, *and make a business of it?*

I knew that this ultralight aircraft was going to be the next big thing and I wanted to be part of it. People had always wanted to conquer slow flight, and I was seeing it happen before my eyes.

From that day forward, my life would not be the same. The years of attempting to build hang gliders that never flew (nearly kill-

44

ing me in the process of testing them) would now come to an end. I would buy an ultralight.

While watching a demonstration in a nearby farmer's field, I met an individual by the name of Stan. Stan would later become a close friend and would play a role in my first successful liftoff.

After purchasing the aircraft, we arrived at the special field where I would receive my first lesson. The training schedule for the day was to taxi up and down the field at no more than ten to twelve miles per hour.

"Get to know the plane first, Hank—practice steering and throttle control."

I buckled up, while Stan pulled the lawnmower-style rope starter. The throttle immediately felt familiar, much the same as the dirt bikes that I rode as a kid.

Stan reminded me that if the wind picked up or I overshot my speed, the plane would begin to lift. "If this happens, immediately shut everything down. Do not attempt a liftoff." The actual flying lesson was to begin in a few days.

Slightly frightened by the responsibility, I made my way down the thousand-foot cornfield runway with caution. Ultralights weigh approximately 150 pounds; they are flown solo and have a wingspan of 36 feet. Their glide ratio is 17 to 1, which means that they will glide seventeen feet for every foot of drop. Their main feature is that they are stall-proof, making them very safe, providing that nothing breaks apart. They're much like a parachute. Stan, now running alongside the aircraft yelling out directions, soon gave up and walked back to the driveway. He was extremely concerned.

I had taxied at least 500 feet now and felt somewhat comfortable with the steering. I took the speed up to the point where Stan had said the front wheels would begin to lift. My thought from the beginning was to let up immediately as Stan had said; but once the wheels lifted ever so slightly, I just couldn't bring them down. It was as if I had lived for that moment in time. For some reason, the idea of parting from the earth had consumed much of my imagination as a child. I felt an absence of fear, mixed with adrenaline. There was a strong impression of tranquility when I was off the turf. The wheels stayed about one foot above the grassy pasture, and I held it there until I felt I had everything under control. I turned around at the end of the runway and took the aircraft up to the two-foot level. This time I kept it there comfortably for at least five hundred feet.

Stan was furious with me when I finally landed back on the runway. He made me promise not to lift off any higher until I'd practiced the landing and takeoff procedure as we had discussed earlier. I agreed with him, and I turned again to the runway to practice my taxiing.

Once in the plane, taxiing on the runway, without thinking, I felt the urge to bring the craft to the takeoff speed of 18 miles per hour. I did the math in my head. If the headwinds were just three miles per hour, my craft would lift off at the same speed as a gentle jog. My landing wheels, anticipating their final release, would ride the smooth air in a fantasy of pleasure. I continued down the field.

Suddenly, I was flying! The warm wind caressed my face, welcoming me to the skies. The small twin-engine, single-propeller power train thrust me ever higher until I felt one with the sky. Now about fifty feet in the air, I made the decision to see if I could control a turn. I had read many books about flight, and when you begin a turn, one wing slows down and loses its lift while the other continues to lift. To compensate for this issue, you must increase power and pull the nose up. The turn was successful; I had understood correctly. Upon my approach, I landed the craft like a professional.

Still buzzing with energy, I made my way back toward Stan. From a distance, I could hear cursing and shouting. "You scared me half to death—you could have caused a disaster."

Stan was right: my wing span was too wide for a fifty-foot-altitude turn. When banking, my wings had come mighty close to the ground. I was too low for the turn; however, Stan said he had never seen a student learn to fly in one hour. Looking squarely in my face, he mumbled something to the effect that there was nothing left for him to do. I had performed a perfect takeoff and landing, together with a controlled turn. The lesson was over. I was a natural.

I furthered my flying skills the following year in Albuquerque, New Mexico, where I received my US ultralight aircraft license. Brian Alan, winner of the first manpowered flight across the English Channel, was involved as my instructor. Brian and his friend Larry Neuman built the first light aircraft, called the Albatross Eagle II. They won the £250,000 reward for the first manpowered flight across the English Channel, which made them world famous. Larry later became one of America's largest builders of ultralights: the Eagle Ultralight.

We thought the whole world would be flying machines like this within ten years. Little did we know that this new invention would create its own nightmare, people were being killed, falling out of the skies. They thought ultralights were toys. Eventually, lawsuits drove Larry Neuman and his company out of business. Great people, great invention, poor timing.

Lightweight aircraft and slow flight had always been an aviator's dream. It's the closest thing to floating on air. What a special time in aviation history to be alive. Wasn't I the lucky one?

I decided to sell ultralights in our retail store. Creating a business from my hobby might not have been the best choice, but I did it anyway. I was a salesman, and I knew I could sell anything to my friends. It was a perfect fit. I had my instructor's license, and I already had a retail store called a Recreation Centre. The stage was set. All I had to do was bring in the ultralights and put them on display. We showed videos in the store and in the local shopping malls on how easy it was to fly. The local parachute centre's airstrip was our training facility. We were now in business.

Our first year with the lightweight aircraft was a hit. Enthusiasm and customer demand was high. By the end of the third year, I had sold over sixty-five ultralights and trained customers how to fly and become pilots. In the '80s, they sold for $4,000 to $6,000. Today they start at $25,000 and higher. There were no regulations. We could land in any schoolyard, fly under bridges, and visit our friends in the country.

I remember a time in Albuquerque when I saw an illegal flight. Larry Neuman (the inventor of the Eagle Ultralight) rolled the craft out of the garage bay door, warmed up the engine, and flew away. He happened to have been featured on the American Express credit card commercial; he was the city's celebrity representative for their slogan of "Don't Leave Home Without It." Nobody but Larry could have gotten away with taxiing an ultralight down the narrow back lane, then slowly flying over the neighboring commercial buildings. The climax came when he actually landed on the roof of his factory, with about ten feet to spare. Passersby, along with me, had never seen anything so bizarre.

I remember the day when I got the telephone call. Wayne Elias, my old school friend, had crashed the plane during training. It was my company's plane, and I knew it would be totaled; but the important question was whether he was dead or alive. He was alive and unhurt. He had rotated during his tow rope landing. In other words, he overreacted, panicked, and ended up overcompensating his flight controls. It was Elias's last attempt to fly; and as disappointing as it was, once you learn you have the personality to panic under pressure, you become afraid. Wayne had panicked, and it nearly cost him his life.

Shortly after this experience, I took the opportunity to sell the ultralight business to a friend in aviation. I could no longer handle the risk.

6 The Power Thought

Here is where Rover ends and the Cap-it story begins. I don't know if you have ever heard Robert Schuller's term for a life-changing experience—*power thought*. I certainly had one. To this day, I'm not certain where it came from. Was it fate? All I know is that this *power thought* did change my life forever. In some remote place in my mind, I believe that *power thoughts* are the Creator's way of directing you in your life.

The power thought was: *We're going to franchise our business.*

We had been in business for thirteen years up until then, operating under the Rover name. After deciding to franchise our concept, we were advised to register our name as franchise law requires and get it trademarked. However, Land Rover of England had already trademarked their name for everything and anything automotive, making it impossible for us to use the name in our new franchise. We were very disappointed. *Rover* had become well known in our community and had developed a great reputation. What were we to do? After many months, we came up with an idea: if you have a truck, we will cap it. It came from the term *truck cap* (truck canopy)

We called our new company Cap-it. I remember answering the telephone the next day: "Cap-it, good morning, how can I help you?" It felt odd; no one had ever heard the name *Cap-it* in our town.

I was on top of the world, spending the weekend with my wife in Vancouver's most luxurious and expensive hotel. I surfaced from sleep, gently coming to consciousness. I opened my eyes to the bright morning. I lay still, strengthened by the increasing light. I pushed off the covers and walked to the window of our Pan Pacific Hotel suite, and saw the magnificent view overlooking Coal Harbour. As I gazed beyond the landscape, my father's life flashed through my mind. He had never had an opportunity to stay in a hotel like this; his goals were only to survive. He did not have the privilege of the education I had, and I know that he made sure I got it. I was fortunate. I wanted to do the best I could in life, and I knew he would be proud of me.

Later, Elaine and I took the elevator to the main floor and went down the long escalator to the restaurant. By this time, the thought had already entered my mind. It was the *power thought.* As if it were life's highest calling, I asked Elaine. "What do you think if we franchise our business?"

Somewhat bewildered, she asked me to repeat the question. Salesman that I am, I went on and convinced her of the wonderful benefits of opening lots of truck canopy and accessory stores like ours.

Yes, we decided to franchise our little truck canopy store; and some five years later, I regretted it more than anything I had ever done in my life. But at that moment, the thought of developing the franchise idea and taking it to the marketplace was electrifying! My wife and I could see ourselves teaching others how to build and run a successful business. We would take everything that we had learned during the last thirteen years and help teach others what not to do. We had made mistakes and would now use the experience and our expertise to prevent others from taking the wrong turns down the same road.

Our goal was honorable. It was not for riches or for an easier life but a way that we could help others. Many a future day would come when I would search my heart for any other motive that might have been hidden, especially the days when things were not so good.

God must have been in this plan because everything came together. The first thing I did was to visit a good friend who was my age, Ron Martens, owner of one of Western Canada's largest restaurant chains, ABC Country Restaurants, now operated by the Ricky's chain of restaurants. I told him what I was preparing to do, and with much encouragement from Ron, we moved ahead.

Among several things he commented on, he suggested that I make sure there was sufficient royalty revenue in the NAF (National Advertising Fund); he had just gone through an ordeal with his franchisees in changing this fund, so he recommended that I not make the same mistake. Also, he gave me the name of a man who would help us to get going and eventually become the one man who could put us on the map: Norm Friend.

The following week, I met Norm Friend at Vancouver's Pacific Franchise Trade Show. Without a description to go by, I immediately picked him out of the crowd. He looked professional, and he had the gift of spinning tales and creating interest. I was drawn to the most unusual (and I thought inappropriate) theme one could speak on at a trade show. The sign in front of his stage read, "Which Franchises Not to Buy." A title like that, particularly at a franchise show, got everyone's attention. He delivered a riveting, sidewalk salesmanship message.

Elaine and I were immediately impressed. He spoke extensively on the topic, and was easy to listen to. Norm recommended companies with thick (comprehensive) franchise agreements that created absolute control. "They're better for you," he explained. The franchises *not to buy* were the ones that had thin (short) franchise agreements; those agreements gave little or no protection to the franchisees.

He went on to explain that should any franchisee in the group cause difficulties that will also affect other franchisees' stores, the franchisor must have the proper instruments in place to deal with the matter legally. The big franchisors attending the show applauded him for the fact that his approach made sense to them.

As qualified as he was, Norm Friend should have been running his own franchise. He had talent, and he knew it; the only problem was that he couldn't figure out why he wasn't as profitable as some of the companies he was advising.

What impressed me most about Norm Friend was that he had a sales pitch that rivaled mine. Norm impressed people when he spoke. I call it communication skills; he had a presence about him and the talent to express an idea like no one else. Crowds would stop in their tracks and listen when he was speaking. Under his tutelage, I began my journey into the land of franchising. Understanding franchise law, systems, and terms:

- We're not here to sell franchises, we award them
- It's perceived value that counts
- And directed to the franchisors: "If they succeed, they've done it; if they fail, we've done it."

I had cracked open a fortune cookie: You are going to succeed in your new adventure.

Norm and I felt comfortable with each other from the beginning, as if we were made for one another. He painted word pictures similar to the scenes that had flashed across my mind earlier. I was impressed with the community of businessmen Norm worked with. He would mention business leaders like Vancouver's real estate mogul, Peter Thomas of Century 21, who sought his advice and so on. Friend continued to impress me. I thought that we had the same dream, as it turned out in the end, we didn't; nevertheless, I couldn't have franchised the business without him.

Franchise, you ask? Why not? Most of the largest companies in the world were franchised. And besides, franchising is the fastest way to grow, because you don't have to use your own money to do it—at least that's what I thought in the beginning at the age of forty-two. In general, people want to belong to an organization and be connected to someone in case they need help.

As Friend began interviewing me, he established the fact that Cap-it met all the criteria required to start a franchise. We had been in the same business for thirteen years, we had a low-entry cost, we had a proven success story, and we came from a fragmented industry. We had a nuts-and-bolts business. Unlike other retailers in our business, we installed everything we sold.

Friend spoke to me about how he had attained his reputation. He was good at marketing. He had been employed by some of BC's finest franchise firms. As president of the Pacific Franchise

Association, he knew just about everyone in the industry. He was involved with the Speakers Bureau of Vancouver, and did the circuit from time to time, accepting speaking engagements across the United States and Canada. Not long afterward, Friend joined our company and worked for us in Abbotsford as executive director of operations.

It was 1992, and we were on a roll. *The Vancouver Sun* ran a full page-and-a-half on how we became the fastest-growing franchise in BC. *Business in Vancouver* also ran several large editorials describing how Hank Funk had developed a system in the truck canopy industry that investors should know about.

"Good profits with small investment."

"Funk system paves the way for franchisees."

Setting up New Franchise Locations

We had a great strategy for finding the right location for a new franchise. It was all about the people who lived in the town and how many trucks there were, compared to cars. Elaine and I would drive our truck to various locations in the Lower Mainland, including Vancouver Island, in search of the best and most economical sites that we could rent for as little as $3,000 per month. Rent higher than that was out of the question.

We parked on the roadside at 11:00 a.m. and at 4:00 p.m., taking ten-minute traffic counts. We chose the 11:00eleven o'clock time because we didn't want noon-hour traffic. and we chose the 4:00four o'clock time because we didn't want rush-hour traffic. We wanted local traffic, but not commuters. It was all about getting to know the different communities and the percentage of trucks that they supported.

We counted all the trucks and all the cars. If the percentage came out to be 38% light pick-up trucks compared to 62% cars—, we considered that a likely community in which to place a Cap-it store. Despite the fact that one million people lived there, areas like Kingsway Street in Burnaby averaged only 4% trucks, so we didn't consider locating a store there. Currently, we take SUVs (sport utility vehicles) and vans into consideration when considering a location. We now look for at least a 35%-50% ratio pick-up trucks, SUVs, and vans compared to cars. Some cities in Alberta can be well over 65%. Age of the population, average income, and total population are now all factors that we consider in choosing the right location for a new store.

We opened five stores in one year, in addition to the original two. We were featured in many magazines across North America, all speaking about our success. I knew that some of the editorials were saying things that were not true. Most editorial writers had embellished the facts, no matter how clear I had been during the interview. To say we didn't enjoy reading our own headlines would be a lie, but no matter how many times I told others that we were very small and only had seven stores, readers wanted to believe the headlines. "If it's in print, it must be true."

Today, when interviewing applicants, I look back on that time, and I ask them big-picture questions. "What stage of life are you in? Why do you want to risk all your money in a business?" After a careful analysis of their situation, I try to help them make the right decision. I warn them of pitfalls they may not be prepared for.

Absorbed by an overwhelming sense of accomplishment and the attraction of success, I pushed ahead. The pitch of my voice rose each time I spoke of franchising. I had the passion, and I knew it. It would overcome any talent I was missing, and besides, I had faith; it had always worked for me before.

Franchising would consume my whole life. After opening our first seven stores, I got the phone call. No one had ever seen a truck accessory store setup like ours. Our stores had beautiful displays. I'm an artist by nature, and store design came naturally.

News had gotten out, and with our permission, our video tape had crossed the desks of some important people in the United States. I was asked to fly to Las Vegas and meet with President Dick Cassiopeia of LEER West, the leading manufacturer of truck caps on the Coast.

I remember the meeting in Las Vegas. There were seven of us present to discuss the possibilities of joint venturing. We met at Bally's Hotel, in the hospitality suite on the thirtieth floor. Las Vegas, bustling as ever, was entertaining the 30,000 Specialty Equipment Market Association (SEMA) attendees. The view from the window was breathtaking. But this time the Vegas main strip below appeared to be frozen in time. The room was silent; each of us pondered the questions we posed to one another. None of us knew what to expect from the discussion, but we all knew that something would come together.

We needed each other—LEER was our largest manufacturer and supplier, and we were one of their largest customers. Dick was honest and admitted they didn't have a clue how to run retail. They admired our sophisticated retail truck store setup, and wondered if we could do it for them. Cassiopeia was responsible for LEER's retail division. Impressed with what we had accomplished, he asked me to help them manage the opening and operation of their American stores.

Several months after the meeting, I flew to Atlanta, Georgia. I remember that night in Atlanta, alone in my room, still trying to catch some sleep before the early-morning flight back home. I sat up in bed. Tossing and turning wasn't helping; I had to deal with it sooner or later, and it might as well be now. By this time, I had visions of great things, but the results of the late-afternoon meeting said otherwise. I was disappointed and saddened. I wasn't looking for a job; I was looking to sell them our franchise system.

After many weeks and months, the owner of LEER rejected our plan to franchise. They thought the difficulties in overcoming state security regulations and federal pricing regulations outweighed the benefits. They elected to grow by owning their own stores. The great franchise opportunity ended there. My ego was hurt, and I castigated myself for not realizing earlier in the plan that it might not happen. I was my own worst enemy. I had set myself up.

I had seven operating stores, and I knew that I needed time and money to accomplish what was ahead of me. The merger with

LEER would provide me the time and the money to hire the necessary people to accomplish the services we so desperately needed. I knew that there were things ahead of us that still needed to be solved and accomplished. I was hoping that the LEER deal would give me additional stores in our early days of franchising. It's a big task to cater to the needs of every franchisee, especially ones that are not knowledgeable on the basics of business. In addition, the LEER deal would have provided us the clout and credibility that would have been essential for a quicker step toward the recognition we needed in opening more stores.

The Principles of Retailing

Some years later, we received a call from LEER, asking if we were interested in purchasing their remaining 14 stores. They had opened approximately 35 stores and managed the warehouse and supplied them all but wanted to get out of retail. The decision not to purchase the 14 stores was made with great reluctance. I was tired taking on partners, and flying around the country didn't appeal to me as it had in prior years.

I had said it from the beginning: it's difficult for a manufacturer to run successful retail stores, just as it would be for us to begin manufacturing our own truck caps. It takes a lot of knowledge and expertise in these specific fields. There are just too many things you need to know if you are going to succeed. Our industry was just too young; no one had ever done it, it just took LEER time to realize that. Today LEER has become the largest truck cap manufacturer in North America, with many facilities across the country, and they're leaving the retailing to others.

I believe there were several things that led Leer to shut down their retail network. LEER manufactured truck caps and covers and would sell direct to their own stores but had to rely on outside suppliers for the truck accessories side, which represents over 50% of the business. Distribution was a problem for Leer. Today, publicly owned distribution companies such as Keystone Distributors provide truck accessories at Jobber (wholesale) pricing and next-day service to independent store owners. Back in those days, you had to do it by yourself; the Keystones had not yet been realized.

Today independent businesses rely on these warehouses to supply them daily. However, these independents are purchasing at Jobber pricing, giving the warehouses a good margin of profit even at wholesale. You can't buy from these warehouses if you plan on being competitive with big-box stores, or if you have a chain of stores like ours.

Leer began setting up huge warehouse distribution centres to supply truck accessories to their own stores, a step that is not cost efficient in today's supply chain. A warehouse cannot be a part of the line of supply unless its managed correctly. Dead inventory is your first enemy and if you don't have a proper category management system in place that manages this, all your profits go up in smoke. Warehouses must make a margin, which is proper business, but in a supply chain system such as Cap-it, margins are extremely small. The focus and profitability is always toward the stores success so the warehouse must sell to franchisees on a cost plus-bases, in general lower than Jobber pricing. The real goal is to bypass the middleman (the Keystones) whenever possible. Particularly if you have a chain of stores where you must compete with the independents and big-box stores.

Today most big-box stores buy their product direct from manufactures, bypassing the warehouses or if anything flows through their warehouses, at little or no margin.

Secondly, staffing and training people is a business of its own. Managers may not show up for work, and they may not pay attention to the details. Why should they? They don't own the store, and do they really care as much as an owner? Whereas in the franchising world, each store has an owner, an operator that is always there. After all, nobody cares more for a store than its owner.

And thirdly, you have to have a team of retail people specializing in business intelligence just to handle the day-to-day business, accounting, marketing, research, and development and so on.

Back in 1993 our seven stores demanded the service only a small army of trained professionals could provide. Although we might have been happy at first with the purchase of LEER's other stores, I knew that I alone couldn't provide them with the expertise they needed, nor could I afford to hire the required staff. By now, I had accumulated enough cash to be somewhat comfortable, and I decided to invest it all in building and improving our *own* system.

Funding The Business

Everyone knew and understood that Cap-it was in the beginning stages as a franchise. The appealing little store with the relatively low buy-in attracted many frustrated employees, giving them hope of someday owning their own business. We could sell as many franchises as we cared to open. The problem was that we encountered many setbacks in the third year, and found it difficult. I had run three of my own profitable and successful stores for many years. I didn't know why the new franchisees had such difficulties. We decided to proceed cautiously in examining the problems with the new stores. In order to analyze the situation and regroup, we immediately held off from opening more stores.

First, we decided to select applicants with sufficient, unencumbered cash and who owned their own home. We would not accept just anyone. Secondly, they had to have some business skills, be energetic, enthusiastic, and have a great personality. And thirdly, we wanted people who knew the importance of following the Cap-it system. Their success depended on it.

We were determined to include two important ingredients for our new franchisees: onsite training and ongoing education. Often, we had to educate first-time buyers how to perform the basic operations of business. The next time we opened a store, we would insist on staffing it with our own people until the franchisee was able to take over. And time would help us to find that pivotal and key component that would set us apart from other independents.

Realizing that money could buy this much-needed time, I inquired from the best advisors about what to do next. I considered taking my company public. I was introduced to a wonderful man, someone who deserves mentioning here—Ron Klassen, a securities lawyer in Vancouver.

A lot of Canadian franchises at that time came from Vancouver. On the occasion of my first meeting with Klassen, it was pure pleasure to park the car and walk toward the brick tower where his office was located, listening to the hustle of the city. As if the city was a museum, I continued to absorb my surroundings, trying to collect everything this day had to offer.

The appointment had been made, and I was determined to find the necessary money for follow-through. Klassen and I spent several hours discussing the pros and cons of taking our company public. Our concept was eligible for venture capital funding, and taking it public would be easy. As Klassen spoke, I sensed an intelligent, caring man. The horror stories of corporate boardrooms and the disappointment of losing control brought shivers to my once-hopeful heart. I had expertise in retail, and I knew I could easily be out of my league in this world. Somewhat sad and somewhat grateful, I walked away. Another door closed. The words from entrepreneur Nelson Skalbania, cited in a book I had read earlier came back to me: "There are only two reasons to go public: either you're broke or you're stupid."

In 1994, I ended up selling a small percentage of my company privately to raise cash. Bill Fast, an acquaintance of mine, lived in Abbotsford and wanted to buy a minority share position in Cap-it. This came at a much-needed time. I didn't want to have any partners after my experience back in the 1970s, but Bill was a nice man with a great local reputation. I thought it would work for him and for our company.

We wanted to expand into Alberta, which had the reputation of higher truck canopy sales than the province of BC, and we thought that this would be the place for us to expand. However, being a franchise, we had to first pass Alberta franchise disclosure law. The cost to do this was $80,000, money we didn't have; and so part of Bill's money would go toward this.

Learning the Distribution System

In 1992, we moved our headquarters to a larger office on Townline Road in Abbotsford BC, a short distance from our main retail store. It was twice the size of the one we had in the KPMG building in Abbotsford the year we started in 1990, and it included a very small warehouse. It had a beautiful new large office, and we could now hire professional bookkeeping help.

My wife, Elaine, had managed all our accounting from the beginning. I still remember watching her doing the bookkeeping in the early years while raising our two boys. There was always a baby crib close to her office desk. Time had passed, and there would be no baby crib in this new office.

Having our own warehouse space led us to a totally new set of problems. Warehousing space allowed us to hold on to a lot of dead inventory. We couldn't return it to our suppliers. Some of our franchisees couldn't or wouldn't pay their bills on time, which made us their bankers in some cases—something we had not planned on.

A few of the franchisees could always come up with some excuse as to why they couldn't pay for their orders on time. We had just been too patient and kind at the time, and couldn't afford to continue that behavior.

We were advised by other people in the franchise industry to find an outside supplier who would supply our stores and let those suppliers hold the accounts receivable and deal with the franchisees and the accounts receivable.

The initial advice I got was to follow the muffler business; after all, they were automotive. Why not? The muffler business had a local warehouse that inventoried all their muffler parts and sold to the Budget Brakes, Speedy Muffler, and the Midas stores and so on, why not give that system a try?

And so we started an alliance with a local distributor. We had to get out of the warehouse business. We needed money and better buying power as well. We began to purchase product from a local accessory distributor in Langley (Lyco Products) that gave us a small discount, considering the volume of purchases we were giving them annually. However, as the company grew from just selling truck canopies, the truck accessory market exploded, increasing our badly needed sales revenue. The problem was that the discounts we were receiving on accessories were not enough. We found out that a competitor of ours in Alberta, with only 7 stores, owned their own warehouse and sold to their own stores at a very small percentage over cost. They were more competitive than we were because of this; it appeared that they had figured it out. I wanted to learn more. How did they do it?

The time had come, and I recognized it (maybe one of my survival skills). I knew that I had to provide better pricing to the franchisees, or we would not survive. What was I to do? Find a better source to purchase our products, a source that would sell to us at a small percentage above cost. Who would do that?

The source turned out to be the warehouse in Alberta: the Truck Outfitters. If I could make a deal with them, our franchisees would be able to buy product at much lower pricing. We could then compete with the big-box retailers. But how would we do a deal with the Outfitters, was the question. They *were* our competitor.

We realized that opening more stores in our situation had the potential to be disastrous. The original plan had called for us to wait a year or two until we had more infrastructure in place and a better source of supply. At that time, we had seven stores. So we shut down our very small warehouse on Townline Road, Abbotsford, and moved the head office into our home.

We also found out that our current supplier, Lyco Products, with whom we had chosen to form the strategic alliance, didn't work out. The owner died and had left the business to his son, who didn't have a good grasp of the value that Cap-it brought to the table. We had guaranteed them $1 million in purchases per year in favor of better pricing.

The strategic alliance worked for approximately two years, a short period of time. Things began to unravel when Lyco began to sell to our competitor for much the same price as ours and then there were times when we were threatened to buy more in an effort to keep the pricing alliance together.

Later we realized that warehousing had to be a part of the franchise system. It would play an integral role in our future, we needed better supply and pricing

7 Truck Cap Misadventures

Another one of my earliest strategies had been to introduce a plastic truck cap for the Canadian market. Something I knew no one else had done. Something that could be the beginning of the magic that I needed for the fledgling franchise system.

If you walked through a conventional fiberglass manufacturing facility, the stench of harsh chemicals, together with the sticky mess of molding fiberglass, would have seemed as old-fashioned as forming bricks by hand. Everything seems to be made of plastic—why not a canopy? With the new emission control regulations about to be announced it seemed, thermal vacuum-forming of plastics would soon become the new way.

At the time, a double-platinum vacuum-forming machine cost approximately US$250,000 per unit, and had to be hand-built. Stretching hot plastic around large, tub-shaped molds was a new technology. Plastic composite looked to be the way of the future, and I wanted to be part of it. It was beautiful to see a perfectly flat white sheet of plastic formed into a canopy in mere minutes. Nowadays, it seemed that everything was made from plastic—why not a truck cap? At least that's what we thought.

The Canadian market was fiberglass-driven, and the forward-thinking Yankees, BacPac Industries of California, were beginning to produce the new plastic-formed truck caps in big numbers. Their in-store sales video presented an image of toughness. Our sales pitch was the best. Nine out of ten customers preferred our plastic canopies to our competitor's fiberglass units.

You could hit the plastic truck cap with a heavy piece of timber, and it wouldn't break. You could throw it off a cliff, and it wouldn't break. You could drag it behind a vehicle on a dirt track through the back roads and put it right back on your truck, dusty but indestructible.

By the second year of selling these new plastic truck caps, we were the largest distributor/retailer of Bac-Pac plastic truck caps. Any time you can make an improvement to the industry, you are in a position to profit, and we did. It couldn't have been better timing: we had just started franchising, and we were making staggering inroads into the Canadian truck cap market. I thought my dreams were coming true. BacPac was perfect. No one would ever consider buying a fiberglass truck after seeing this sales video.

In 1990, a custom-painted truck cap sold for around $1,395—a considerable sum. Truck caps were our flagship product and represented 50-60% of our product mix. A unique and perfect product to help build the franchise network.

A plastic truck cap could now be formed in seven minutes through the process of vacuum-forming. It looked new, and appeared to be totally acceptable as a newly invented product. It seemed to answer everyone's needs. We sold it as unbreakable and indestructible, and it was beginning to affect the reputation of the old fiberglass canopies that our competitors manufactured and sold. It was the hottest truck cap in the industry, and Cap-it was the only company in Canada that sold it.

Two years later, somewhat relieved after my quarterly visit to our Kelowna store, I drove away knowing that what we were experiencing was only a small hurdle, much like others we'd experienced before. Like all the other problems, we would get through this one. I was confident that all would be well. There were cracks appearing in our plastic truck caps. We could handle it.

Our new "unbreakable" truck cap was breaking. So far, sixteen canopies had cracked at the side window and by the back door. It wasn't a freak accident or a poorly manufactured product, but these returns were beginning to occur on a weekly basis. Customers came back to the Cap-it stores slightly embarrassed for our sake, trying to show us the unimaginable crack. They knew that we would take care of them.

Our suppliers had assured us that they would replace all the broken truck caps with the new, stronger, more reliable Rovel plastic material, made with a higher, more elastic rubber content.

Customers began to identify with the new Rovel (plastic composite) product because it did much more than anything they had ever seen. It was the edge we needed. I wanted our franchise to be on the leading edge, and I believed that the Rovel truck cap was the ticket to building a successful franchise.

Most of Canada's truck cap manufacturers were located in the small town of Summerland, in BC's interior. We had set up our sixth store in that general area, knowing that we could definitely compete with our imported canopies, no matter how difficult it might seem; we had something different to offer the customer, and we knew that the customer would pay the difference. Our Abbotsford and Surrey stores had proven this by now.

But soon, we desperately needed to find a replacement for the "unbreakable" Bac-Pac plastic truck cap that we were selling. This truck cap was the product that we had hoped would take us into the future, but they were breaking by the hundreds, and we needed to find a replacement, fast. But *how?* In the back of my mind, I had always believed that my faith would provide, but that didn't seem to be working.

The first year, we had 250 units come back. Monsanto had been the original manufacturer of the plastic Rovel Pellets that were used to extrude the flat white sheets. They had accepted responsibility for all the breakage problems. A year later, the new supplier, Dow Chemical, convinced Bac-Pac that they had solved the breakage problem by improving the formula. They were now adding the badly needed rubber content. This would prevent the shrinkage that occurred when temperatures dropped below -23 Celsius and stop the cracking at the windows and back doors.

Another year later, an additional 300 units were broken. By now, customers were coming in every other day complaining that their replacement canopies were cracking too.

When it was all over, we had 550 units come back. Eventually, Monsanto did replace the first 250 broken units so we could keep our customers happy. But Dow Chemical never did replace any of the 300 units. They claimed it was BacPac's fault for incorrect assembly. Talk about a setback. As Eric Thomas wrote in *The Secret to Success*, "A setback is a setup for a comeback." Those words are easy to say when it's all over and ten years later. The smooth path of our great beginning had not prepared us for the rocky road we now encountered. My franchising had been based on our secret weapon: the vacuum-formed plastic canopy. And with our secret weapon imploding, we would be on a much weaker footing compared with our competitors. I couldn't see how we could possibly grow the franchise by selling fiberglass canopies. I was devastated.

Despite my valiant thoughts about the breakage dilemma, I was not prepared for what appeared to lie ahead. Was this situation a test of my abilities, or was it telling me I had made a terrible mistake building a franchise system on the plastic truck cap? Maybe I intended to carry on with respect for the others who had passed this way before. Maybe it was destiny, but I knew one thing—it was my turn now, and I had to solve this problem. I wasn't prepared for such catastrophic failure of my franchise system. Nobody would think that in this day and age, a plastic product would break. Couldn't someone figure out what the problem was? After all, they manufactured spas and hot tubs out of the same material, and still do to this day. Why the truck cap—my prized truck cap was cracking?

Looking back on it, it appears relatively commonplace; but back then, it was absolute despair. Today, earth-shattering problems are dealt with using the same, everyday problem-solving strategies; we solve each problem as it comes along, one at a time.

I felt strongly that we had an edge over the competition. The basic concept of franchising is that you possess one or more ingredients that give you an advantage. It is for this reason that franchising is one of Canada's fastest growing industries. I had begun franchising knowing full well that there would be areas where I'd have to improve; it was only natural.

Franchise organizations can be enormously successful. They develop better-tasting or longer-lasting products, simplify systems, and give faster service—all in an effort to get greater market share. They do it well, they're professional, and they can make more money. Successful franchises can usually outperform independent business.

Franchises are successful because they have created a time-tested and well-developed system for running a business. This system takes in to account all aspects of running a successful franchise, and nothing is left to chance.

Since the system is so critical to the success of the franchisee, franchisors offer their franchisees excellent training and very close support during the life of the franchise relationship. Sometimes franchisees get frustrated because franchisors offer very little leeway in the way things are done, but franchisees must understand that this is done for the good of both the individual franchisee and the overall franchise organization.

What were we meant to do? By this time, many people had bought our franchise system, creating even more responsibility. A huge weight had fallen on me, and I had nowhere to run.

On several occasions, Elaine and I were invited to the home of one of our franchisees for dinner. Their respect for us was genuine, and as we continued to visit, my mind drifted back to the real problems that lay before them. We felt the pressure of their financial pressures. Losing your own money is one thing, but seeing others lose theirs because they believed in you is another. The pain was overwhelming.

Taunted by the successes of my friends and the failures of my ideas, I was close to slipping into depression. The weight at times was unbearable, and even though I prayed to the point of begging, the disasters continued coming.

It was another one of those cold wet weeks where we experienced the monsoons. Day after day, the rain was driven sideways by the raging winds. Low, dark-gray clouds dumped rain as they sailed past the office window. Feeling as outrageous as the weather, I walked out toward the ocean one day and stood defiantly in the storm. Looking up to the sky while rain pelted my face, my thought was, what was I doing here?

What had brought me to this point of frustration? Why was I so angry?

Without warning, an overwhelming feeling of comfort came over me as I watched the seagulls. During the storm, they waited patiently, huddling close to the ground, for the storm to pass, feathers facing into the wind. While watching them, I realized that I too was part of nature. I would wait for the troubles to pass just like the storm.

We had to bring a case against the BacPac Manufacturing Company. And in addition, BacPac sued Monsanto and Dow Chemical.

I had no choice but to sue our manufacture, Bac Pac, for the canopy breakage and financial losses we were experiencing. After all it had a life time warranty. And Bac Pac in turn sued Dow Chemical, their supplier of Rovel. The lawsuit focused on Rovel™ the plastic sheets that Bac Pac used to vacuum-form truck cap shells. The problem was that the Rovel™ sheet did not function in temperatures below freezing. It had been marketed as almost indestructible, a new kind of plastic that could withstand almost any kind of abuse. But the freezing temperatures of Canada and parts of the USA caused it to break. We had been told by others not affiliated, that the plastic did not contain the rubber compound that would allow shrinkage and expansion. But no one really knows why it broke.

The lawsuit took approximately eight years to resolve, and in the end, no one would receive compensation. It was tough for the franchisees and for me. During one of the depositions that I had to attend, I asked if I could speak to the court recorder and tell my side of the story. The lawyers silently glanced at each other, paused a while and abruptly refused. The lawyers were done with the case and had other things on their minds. It was over for them. They were Americans shopping in Canada. Cuban cigars were contraband in the United States, and the American lawyers were determined not to fly back without them. They all said, "It's nothing personal, Hank. It's just business."

We got ourselves through the BacPac breakage problem. Even though the plastic cap had developed small cracks by the side window, and possibly also by the back doors, the court ruled that the product, for all intents and purposes, carried out the duties it was purchased to do. Explaining this ruling to my customers was a more difficult thing.

We developed two procedures to allow customers to return their truck caps, hundreds of them, for a new cap with the condition that the usage would be prorated. They would be given credit for their truck caps, but we had to deduct the time they had used them. In some cases, the cap was two or three years old. Our other procedure was to give the customer a credit on any other purchase. In many cases, it worked well for us to resell the cracked canopies at a discounted price. And in some cases, customers continued to use their caps in the cracked condition, and those customers never came back.

The BacPacs had been beautiful truck caps. Our stores were able to get through the ordeal fairly well. However, the BacPac manufacturing plant in California went out of business.

We had no other choice than to go back to selling the fiberglass truck caps, knowing full well that competitors would be on much the same price level as us. By now no one was manufacturing the plastic truck cap. Plastic was out of the question, the industry was afraid of what had happened, and we knew that going back to selling fiberglass truck caps would bring its own set of problems.

Canadians had their own manufactures selling fiberglass Caps and everyone was at the same cost level when it came to buying. Cap-it may get a small discount because of its volume but we knew that the freight component being so high, the discount would not be enough to set Cap-it apart from other competitors.

If we bought fiberglass from the Americans we would at least get better style and design, much superior to anything Canadians could offer. Cap-it always looked at setting itself apart from competitors. And so the decision was made to buy fiberglass truck caps from a company called LEER, they tagged themselves "the king of caps" manufactured in Woodland California. They offered a great looking product and design no one had seen in Canada. This was the beginning of a long relationship with Leer. Leer was excited to sell to us because they had never had a dealer in Canada before, let alone a multi store organization like ours.

8 A Difficult Time

It was the early period in my business life when I truly felt I had lost my way. It was almost too late by the time I recognized it. In the beginning, all entrepreneurs must do all the jobs. Starting a franchise with little money and a few staff had forced me to do everything that needed to be done.

I did everything.

I was selling franchises, doing most of the training, decorating, and setting up new stores, conducting store visits, etc. And in addition, I was the president, the marketing manager, and so on. The tide turned, and I felt my integrity was at stake. I no longer had the influence over or confidence of the franchisees that I once had. I found out they didn't want me doing everything. In the first few years, the more successful in some areas that we appeared, the more I changed. Finally, I learned that being myself was what people wanted.

Losing my integrity was like losing my company. It was my dream, and I needed the franchisees to accomplish it. This was a serious loss. What could I do, and how could I get back the respect I once enjoyed? It wasn't that I had become proud or arrogant as a leader. I just wanted to play the role that I had admired so much in other leaders. In my mind, a leader had to look the part, so I dressed and did what I thought people wanted.

Individuals who win lotteries usually end up changing their lives without realizing it, and that's when they lose their friends. Friends want you the way they have always known you. If you become a different person, you may destroy the bonds that held you together

71

in the first place. Realizing this, I made the decision to go back. Not only did I go back to the person everyone once knew and felt comfortable with, but now I had a more humble attitude.

Franchising can be a strange thing: the strength that takes you to the top can also be the instrument that brings you down. In other words, your greatest strength can become your greatest weakness. Catching myself and making corrections as I went along prevented much of the possible damage. Even though I personally feel more comfortable in business attire, I felt it was better to dress to the standards of the industry. I took off my white shirt and tie and replaced them with cowboy boots and jeans.

At least in the early days they didn't want me, the president, doing everything myself; and so I hired more staff to help with the responsibilities and fill the different roles. I became one of them. I learned that people are seldom attracted to individuals that have all the answers; rather, they prefer personalities that listen well.

When you're in the people business, you have to learn how to read people in an effort to close and make the sale. Body language is one example of how to read a customer. You learn to copy their moves, make them feel that you are one of them. What we are effectively doing is getting their acceptance. If you can convince them that you are on the same page, you will get the sale. People feel most comfortable with people who have the same values.

When things don't work in life, it's usually because there are some areas we have no control over. I soon learned that the only thing I actually had control over was me.

I regained the trust that I thought I was losing.

When things don't work in life, it's usually because there are some areas we have no control over. I soon learned that the only thing I actually had control over was me. My wife, our kids, our friends, and my employees all have minds of their own. If there's ever any hope of being the master of your life, you have to understand the differences. A person can only control and master themselves. Sometimes we get confused about our responsibilities: even though we may be responsible for others, it's our self that needs us the most.

The hurdles and difficulties that came along, what appeared to be every day began to take their toll on me. I saw others in business and thought that their life was easier, which added to my frustration. My opinion has always been that when something bad happens, surely it's eventually going to turn out for the better. But I can tell you that a time can come in your life when you begin to feel that there are too many problems occurring at once. The problems begin to overwhelm you, and your positive attitude flies out the window. The year 1994 was such a time. BacPacs were breaking! What good could ever possibly come from this? Why did it happen to my franchisees and me? I wanted to do so much good for them.

I scrambled for the next *power thought*; the *one thing* that would have the power to put things right. Franchisees were depending on me now. In their minds, I knew everything; and if there were problems, it would be my responsibility to fix them. After all, they were paying for my expertise.

There was more bad luck to come. By 1994, the Canadian dollar had weakened, making it virtually impossible to continue to buy from the US and still compete with the Canadian manufacturers. It became evident that buying from United States manufacturers had to come to an end. The Canadian dollar was at 64 cents compared to the US dollar. We were paying up to $1.60 for one American dollar. I had to find a Canadian source quickly. Buying Canadian would put us on the same level as my competitors, and our system would definitely be tested. We had to develop other products or methods that would keep us profitable.

Still able to fight, but without any smart weaponry, I had to advance cautiously. Until now, my confidence had been my firepower; my own drive was the strategy I had chosen to grow the company. Like a good general, I had designed the best battle strategies, selected the best weapons, and, whenever necessary, carefully made adjustments to the plan. I was determined to conquer with what I had left. But what would I fight with now? The American plastic BacPac truck cap had been taken away from us. The thought of continuing to buy the American LEER fiberglass truck cap was out of the question: the cost compared to the same thing made in Canada would be 60% higher. I had to find a Canadian supplier quickly. Win or lose, it was then that I realized what I had left. I had control: control of myself, my own thoughts, and my mind—only myself. Everything around me was apparently controlled by other forces, and if things were to change, the impetus would have to come from me.

I phoned Martin Brown in Drinkwater, Saskatchewan, a Canadian Company, the manufacture of Raider truck caps. Martin was reluctant to sell to us. It took some time to convince him. He already had great representation in the cities and town where we had stores, so I could understand his dilemma. After many days of discussion, the idea of rebranding the same truck caps with a different name on it became our ticket out of the situation we were in. It worked. It saved the day. We now had a reliable Canadian supplier.

During my years in business, I have had the opportunity to meet many people, some have been very wealthy and some not wealthy. The funny thing is that most well-to-do people that I've met, although they may not have had a superior grasp of business, somehow or other managed to be in the right place at the right time. I couldn't find anyone that had similar problems like mine.

You can make a lot of mistakes when you have money and still stay afloat; it can also buy you the time it takes to correct matters. When you don't have money, there's usually very little time. Time is what most people pray for, in addition to wisdom—wisdom to prevent making the mistakes that cost time. I have great respect for the self-made businessperson, and I find that there are few of them around.

The entrepreneurial myth is *you have the same opportunity as Henry Ford had to make millions.* The fact is that the odds of winning the lottery are much better than becoming another Henry Ford. Very few individuals start a business in a garage and then have the ability and knowledge to take it to the next step and become the largest corporation in the world.

One of the best things my parents did for me was to leave me with the impression that I would never amount to much in my life. It made a survivor out of me, and it gave me a desire to achieve and be a winner. After all, what did I have to lose? Anything was better than what I had. I could win.

I was still looking around trying to see who else had experienced what I was going though. I saw that most wealth in North America was controlled by 3 percent of the people, and 95% of this wealth comes from inheritance and is usually lost by the following generations. The remaining percentage comes from privately owned businesses.

I noticed, or at least I felt, that some individuals were always lucky in business. No matter what happened, they always appear to do well while others fail. You could presume that they were born under a lucky star; their sense of timing was always excellent, and they continued to succeed. Eventually, business acumen will determine one's ability to run a company. But in my opinion, timing is the elusive ingredient that we cannot control.

It was at this time that I began to ask for help. I prayed more than I did before. I prayed for everyone by name, each and every day—franchisees, suppliers, my family, and myself. I always had the belief that if God is for you, you can set up your business in the desert, and it will succeed. My success in business and in life will either prove this or disprove it. There have been many times that I had to ask myself, Was God really in this dream of mine? Or was it just my desire? Years passed with no definite answer. As always. Seldom do we get the confirmation we are looking for when we think we need it.

I was sitting at my desk dealing with day-to-day affairs. Up until this moment, business was still a struggle; we were working hard at being creative, still searching for another great idea, when more bad news came. I opened a letter just to find out that someone was suing me for misrepresentation. This was quite a blow, especially when I was working so hard to fix the problems that kept coming up.

This accusation of *misrepresentation* would influence others, taint my reputation, and expose internal problems to my franchisees. I needed time. I had always looked at business as fun, and I intended to keep it that way; but this letter robbed me of every ounce of pleasure I had. After that news, nights were the hardest times, alone with my fragile thoughts, drifting in and out of consciousness. Forsaken and lost, I found myself locked in a dungeon of despair. What could save me from this catastrophic affair? I had never experienced this biting, unrelenting pain and fear in my life before. (The results of the lawsuit are discussed in the chapters ahead.)

Fear handcuffed me. The key to the castle of despair, as John Bunyan put it in *The Pilgrim's Progress,* was hope, the hope that things would improve. Hope would have to be the key to unlock the door and free me from my castle of despair.

It appeared that troubles came with the seasons. Summers were never long enough. Every cold winter felt like the longest winter I could remember. And so it was for many of the beginning years of franchising. Storms blew for at least seven of those years. And after the frigid seasons had ended, I realized I had lost my way. I no longer knew what I wanted or where I was going. I was in a fog. I would get up each morning and go to work not knowing why. I was numb.

> *Hope would have to be the key to unlock the door and free me from my castle of despair.*

I have been told that you can boil a frog without it ever knowing that its demise was coming. It happens so slowly that the frog doesn't even know he is being boiled to death. I now understand how it feels.

The question still remains: *why?* The real answer has never come to me. A good, strong drink may be your way to celebrate your valiant endeavors along the way, and a friend's encouragement will ease the anguish, but the reason why despair settles on you like a fog can never be answered. It's like asking why there's so much starvation and why so many people are dying: we'll never really know the answers. Can it be for a higher cause? If and when an answer does come, it will probably appear late in the game, when it likely won't matter anymore.

To my friends I used to refer to myself as a fireman. I put out fires at work each day. As soon as one fire was extinguished, two more began. Sometimes we were able to find humor in this nickname of mine. My wife reminded me of a comment I made one evening after another blazing fire: "I'm either the smartest man I know, or I'm working with a lot of stupid people." It was not a fair statement.

Of course, my own personality has never made me one that is satisfied with the norm. I always wanted to be the best. I am embarrassed if I am any less, and I realized that someday, there was going to be a price to pay, because everything has its trade-off.

When dealing with problems, solutions tend to move along at their own speed. They have their own momentum, and you can't change it. Once you've done everything that you can to affect the negative situation in a positive way, you must wait patiently for events to unfold. And that's the time to go on holiday.

A big-picture philosophy usually lessens the effects of immediate impending danger. Step back and look at it from a distance. Human nature is to try to solve everything all at once, but that only results in frustration. A good friend of mine always says, "What will it matter a hundred years from now?"

Panic to Power

Unaware of the tumultuous anxiety and fear that encompassed my mind that night, my wife lay there in peaceful sleep. I could never tell her of my weakness; it would take away even more of my self-esteem. It was comforting to know that someone beside me was content, and as an anchor, she portrayed what my heart desired. I wanted to be like her, peaceful and at rest. Someday I'd get over this problem.

Like an army of animals, the relentless pressure of fear came over me, and one more time, I would go into a holding pattern frozen in silence. The very thought of sharing this with someone would, in fact, make things worse. There was an intense anxiety attached to communicating this personal problem with even my closest friend. Was I going nuts? Was I losing my mind? How could I explain this to anyone? Would anyone ever understand what I was trying to say?

I remember an incident: I was taking the customer outside into our truck canopy sales lot to show him a canopy when I passed by the customer's truck. Just by chance and for casual curiosity, I glanced into the cab of the driver's-side window. It was open, and lying on the seat was his dog. It was a yellow Lab, sleeping with its head on the driver's side of the seat, feet out in front, in total calm.

As I passed by, I couldn't help myself. I paused for a split second, and his contented eyes looked at me as if to say something, or nothing. There was no question in his eyes; he was enjoying the moment. The seconds felt like minutes, I remember thinking. At that moment, I envied the spirit and contentment that this animal portrayed. I'll never forget it. I wished I had the peace that dog had.

Today we use terms like *anxiety attack* and *burnout*. They are commonplace, and but in the early eighties, they were not familiar terms. As far as I was concerned, you were either normal or mentally disabled. I believed there was no middle ground. Now forty years later, it appears that many people have experienced some form of burnout or anxiety.

Fear is a terrible thing. It prevented me from thinking rationally, never allowing me to see the unrealistic odds, like ten million to one that any of my fears could ever happen. It robbed me of much joy and happiness during those early years as we raised the kids. Fear saps the very energy that feeds the mind.

Years went by, and with determination and willpower, I decided I wanted to overcome the problem. I searched a lot during those years, continually looking for help and relief. However, my quest for the cure led me to analyze the situation even more carefully. I wanted to be get beyond this anguish. Maybe someone could lead me to the right people, or the right books. I felt that there must be some knowledge of this disease out there, and I wanted to find it.

I took it upon myself to read book after book on personal development—everything I could get my hands on. I trained in the Dale Carnegie program, took the Brian Tracy course, studied at Columbia Bible College, and kept an open mind about any other avenues of personal development. I was on my way to a better life.

The knowledge came slowly and at times appeared that it would never come. My business, although easy to run, appeared to overwhelm me from time to time. The time that I spent away from my business taught me that I did have another life besides the business.

Fear and guilt breed low self-esteem and can rob you of everything that is good. It's like you're unplugged, with no energy to experience life in its fullest.

I remember deciding to take a small piece of paper and write down all the things that I wanted to become, and the dreams I wanted to achieve. This paper would be carried inside my wallet for over ten years, constantly reminding me of what I wanted to be and overcome. This paper eventually became one of the most important tools that helped me recover and achieve my dreams. I wrote down everything I ever wanted to achieve.

Books like *How to Stop Worrying and Start Living* by Dale Carnegie became my go-to books. *The Power of Positive Thinking* by Norman Vincent Peale and *From Panic to Power* by Lucinda Bassett became yet among the first books that led me to a greater understanding of life.

This chapter has been the most difficult for me to write. This is about a time in my life I would sooner forget than try to recollect. The lessons I learned from this ordeal has now become part of who I am. I did get everything I wished for on that list of items I kept in my wallet. And I must add, I have always gotten everything I ever dreamt of having in my life. Anxiety is no longer part of my life, and I've learned how to eat properly, exercise, and live healthy. Also, I've learned that my anxiety came from poor work habits. I was a workaholic. I would work without a break or without food many days. I loved my job. Eating only once a day and then drinking only when I did need a drink, it was a 2-liter bottle of regular Coke. Ask my sons, they'll tell you how I have warned them of the same pitfalls when you enjoy your job and love working that much.

During the darkest years, I found stress relief in other ways. I customized my Harley-Davidson motorcycle, flew my Ultralight aircraft, and built furniture.

If it hadn't been for those bad years, I wouldn't have begun the unstoppable journey in painting in oils either. I never knew I had professional talent in painting until the year I won two awards. In 2001, I won the People's Choice Award in Ellensburg, Washington, together with the Rodeo Poster Artist of the Year award at The National Art Show and Auction in Ellensburg, Washington. If you are traveling through Ellensburg and happen to stop at any of the hotels or restaurants, you will more than likely see my poster hanging on their walls.

The people and store owners of Ellensburg, Washington, have made it a custom to decorate their walls with rodeo poster art. They are very proud of their rodeo heritage; everyone from miles around attend the event. Ellensburg National Fine Art Show & Auction hosts one of the largest collections of western art displayed in the USA during their annual art show. You will see many hotels and restaurants displaying the posters from years gone by. The whole city is in love with their rodeo and the art show.

Ellensburg Rodeo is in its ninety-fourth year, and it's one of America's oldest rodeos and ranked number 4 in the United States for having the largest number of horses in their rodeo parade.

And when you see that 2001 poster, try to look at it as I do. The strong painting with the elegant cowboy was born out of a despondent time in my life—a time that I thought would never end.

9 A Few Good Men

Years later, my wife and I would look back and see the impact certain people made on us as they walked through our doorway. They unknowingly have given us direction as we continued our search through the wilderness of business. One man who walked through our door was like any other sales representative making a sales call. Salespeople were our link to the industry; they kept us informed of current events and presented us with opportunities within the industry. He was well groomed, neat in appearance, and spoke with confidence. I remember Frank Gilfillan, like most good salespeople, walked with an aura of confidence. Our personalities seemed to blend, and we became friends. However, not at first. My hesitation to buy into Gilfillan's sales pitch brought out the best in him. He obviously considered himself a dealmaker, and I, of course, played the devil's advocate. The more resistance he got from me that night, the better he became at his game. Several weeks later, we put the deal together and became authorized dealers for the Glasstite Truck Canopy.

That's what I liked about Gilfillan: he never gave up, and he had his own agenda; and I as a great salesperson was the biggest sucker for a good sales pitch.

Without knowing it at the time, I now see the great impact individuals had on our lives. Those pivotal points left indelible impressions on us and always remind me of the significance of making close friends. I've got to say that I am where I am because of others and their help.

Years later, while on one of our many visits to Kelowna, I asked Gilfillan for some friendly advice. We needed a mature individual to fill the position of operations manager, one who had people skills, business experience, and someone who could be trusted. Our Cap-it franchise was experiencing real growth, and I knew that we would have to get the best in staff as we moved ahead. And so I asked Frank if he would like to join the company and help me build a great franchise organization. I guess it was my turn to give him the sales pitch he couldn't refuse. We had always gotten along very well, trusted each other, and I knew if he became part of our company we could succeed. He had experience with big business and I needed him. Four hours later, he accepted the position.

It was Gilfillan who later on introduced me to Andrew Bilon. He had met Bilon on one of his sales visit to Alberta and pitched him on becoming a Cap-it franchisee. Bilon took the invite and traveled to Kelowna, halfway between Vancouver and Edmonton where Bilon worked and lived.

The meeting took place in a small motel room in Kelowna. Bilon, Gilfillan, and I were discussing the possibilities of how we could blend our two companies and build a bigger organization. Bilon's eight stores in Alberta and my nine stores in BC would give us an edge over the competition.

One small double bed, two chairs, and a twin-sealed window framing the overcrowded parking lot, encompassed us in that tiny room as we debated the hurdles we were to overcome. Bilon is six foot-two inches tall, heavyset, commanding attention by nature, could only sit for short periods at a time. Gilfillan leaning gently against the entry door frame, appearing unfazed by the bantering of experienced business bullshit, lit up a cigarette as to ease the tension that filled the overcrowded room. Each took their position as we battled with our egos. I sat on the bed appearing to be relaxed and trying to moderate the sometimes-heated discussion, taking the neutral position. My intentions, although unnoticed, were always geared toward the close of the deal, which eventually came later in the evening.

Once the initial scrap of who takes first place in the pecking order got established, we were down to business. As franchisors,

Gilfillan and I were selling *perceived value*, while Bilon wanted to pay for *book value* only.

Bathroom breaks and room service lunches were the only moments we had throughout the twelve-hour meeting to catch our breath. Hours later, it eventually came out: Bilon had always dreamed of franchising his own company. He wanted in!

Six months earlier, Gilfillan and I had flown to Edmonton to give Bilon and his two partners, Fred Fishburn and Jim White, our pitch on the merits of franchising the industry. It was during that discussion that Bilon was convinced to come to BC and see for himself how we did what we did. He was hooked, despite his partners' resistance to join in. At one point in the meeting, White gave his three-point rebuttal about the folly of what I was building. It was at that moment, and without thinking, as I had never come across anyone with such a pessimistic attitude, that I shot out, "White, you shouldn't be around a guy like me. You have the ability to destroy anyone's dream."

Who knew that years later I would question whether White knew more about what he was saying than I gave him credit for. Surviving one's dream can be like carrying a heavy cross on one's shoulders. There is a dear price to pay in achieving your dream, and the energy that propels you forward through the adversity maybe the only the reward of seeing your vision come to fruition.

I would always encourage myself by saying things this like, "Men and women who dare to dream dreams must be the greatest in the world. Without them, there would be no Canada or United States to live in freedom, no St. Peter's Basilica or Empire State Building to admire, no songs to soothe or inspire the soul and no commerce to employ people. We are a breed of our own, either gifted or cursed, we must push forward and accomplish as if we were programmed just for the event."

My partner, Bilon, told me that he gave up his marriage in search for fulfillment in business, something I was not prepared to do. In business, he would react to events while I planned for events. Our personalities were opposite, but well placed. His brilliant, well-educated mind, together with his driven personality, combined the necessary body armor we would need as we marched toward our goals. My artistic personality, combined with my unrelenting dream and optimism fueled our need to grow the company.

The answers to my personal struggles were not found in the church, as I had expected, but, rather, at the office. Fate kept sending supplies directly to our office. Through the years, we would meet individuals who would play vital roles in directing our lives.

When I look back my wife and I remember many individuals that walked into our store or just came by to visit. One man in particular was, Mike Feenstra, fund raiser at the Power to Change Ministries organization. I asked him one day, "Mike, how long have you known me" he said I've known you over twenty years, I remember calling on you in the old Surrey store" I hadn't remembered. I said, "I don't remember you ever asking for any donations back in those years". He replied, "I didn't ask because I knew you didn't have the money back then."

I will always be grateful for the all the men, like Mike, that came by to visit, tell of their ministry and encourage me.

10   Constantly on The Move

We opened our first store in Abbotsford in 1977. Our second truck canopy store in Surrey opened in 1984, together with our Poolmart and Dufferin stores 1985. Franchising began in 1990 with a small office in the KPMG building on Simon Avenue in Abbotsford. Our first so-called warehouse was a small forty-foot Atco trailer on the Abbotsford canopy lot in 1988. Our sons, Andrew and Mason, were only fourteen and sixteen years old, and were available to help out in the store after school and on the weekends. Most of the products we sold were truck caps. We sold a few truck accessories.

We relocated the original Surrey store to a better part of town in 1995, five years after we opened. The store was located by the Pattullo Bridge, a swampy side of Surrey beside the Fraser River located in the flood plain. The showroom flooded every time it rained. Quite often, we found ourselves walking in two inches of water in the showroom. The gravel lot got mushy, and the trucks would sink in it up to their hubcaps. We had a difficult time finding properties that had outside storage to accommodate storage of our truck canopies. But after many months, we concluded that if we found a new facility to move to, we would have to store the truck caps inside the showroom.

After months of planning and trying to look into the future, we made a bold decision. We would take a risk and relocate to a side street, off the main highway, out of the way, but in a new strip-mall-style building. There would be no flooding here, and we were located on the newer side of town. However, customers would have to search for us to find us. We called it a "destination location." Fortunately for us, Costco was also opening across the street. It meant that there would be street traffic, but people driving by were unable to see what we sold, because our truck caps were now displayed inside a showroom, something unheard of in our industry. Another first. Cap-it hadn't yet developed its brand name, and few people knew what Cap-it was about. We learned a lot during the moving process. This location required a lot of local advertising, much more than we had done in the past.

It was 1995 when we first opened a 5,000-square-feet warehouse located close to the Surrey store on 178th Street. It was at this time that our son Andrew began to manage the small start-up warehouse he called Western Warehouse with our other son Mason. It couldn't have suited Andrew better, with his precision processor personality that loves numbers. Mason, who had been the head mechanic at the Surrey store, came to me one day, unsettled, and asked if he could be the warehouse road representative. He had spent quite a few years installing truck accessories and was getting tired of it. I couldn't believe it. He had always been the mechanic, and he had such a talent. At first, I didn't want him to leave his position because of this; but at his insistence, I agreed.

I've always been very proud of the boys and our relationship. Not too many dads get to have their sons want to work for them. Since they were young, we always had fun together, and I made sure that we had plenty of fun working together. Yes, the boys had their arguments while at work, but they would often come to me to settle them.

Later on that year, our secretary, Brenda, found a way to get Mason, then our head mechanic, to ask her out on a date. And the rest is history. They were married in 2001 and have three beautiful children.

2003 we moved our warehouse to Gloucester Estates, in Langley BC. We rented a 15,000-square-feet warehouse from the Beedie organization. Coming from a 5,000 square-feet warehouse in Surrey, the new 15,000 square feet gave us plenty of room for growth. Our thoughts were that we'd have at least 10 years before we would have to move to a larger facility. The warehouse was so large that we tried to rent out portion of it as motor home storage. I had made a deal with Ryan Beedie: we would rent the warehouse if he would give me the ability to get out of the lease should we decide to build our own warehouse facility within three years.

This new warehouse was awesome. It gave us a new energy and helped us to focus on expanding our product lines. We learned that purchasing in truck load quantities gave us the extra discounts we needed. Suppliers loved our style and our enthusiasm. Sons, Mason and Andrew were now beginning to play a major role in warehousing. Particularly in procurement, choosing new and up-and-coming products. They were at the right age and could identify what would be a great seller. We found real support from manufacturers; they knew we were capable of merchandizing and marketing their new product lines because we had control over the retail side, unlike other distributors. So much so that we held manufacturers' trade show inside our warehouse. We invited jobbers and franchisees alike to come to the trade show and attend some of the manufacturers' training classes. Everyone could feel the energy.

Three years later, much to our surprise, we ran out of space; and the decision to build our own warehouse became a reality. Beedie followed through and released us from our lease and sold us the land; and we built our new warehouse just down the road from where we were.

The year before we moved, we had a break-in. We were running out of space and decided to rent an additional 5,000 square feet next door as our overflow. Two young physically fit fellows happened to walk into our offices a week before looking for work. They said they were from Newfoundland and needed a job. We hired them as helpers in the warehouse. A week later, we were robbed; the whole 5,000-square-feet space full of inventory had been taken. The police said that the thieves had stolen a five-ton truck down the street and used that to haul away our stuff. We estimated that it took them six hours and many truckloads to get it all out. A total of $65,000 was stolen. We can't prove that those two boys were involved, but they disappeared and never came back for their paychecks. Our product had only been in this new space for about ten days, and the security company had not yet set up the alarm. We guess they figured this out. We were easy pickings. Despite searching for our products on craigslist and flea markets, nothing was ever located. It must have been shipped to another province.

In 2006, the custom built warehouse was the most expensive thing I ever bought in my life, in the millions. How was I going to pay for it? Where would I get the cash for the down payment. Between Elaine and me and the boys, we managed to personally finance the down payment.

I remember the day I went to the construction site and saw the steel roof trusses being set up with cranes. It was a 32,000-square-feet building. I longed for my father that day. He would have enjoyed walking through the building with me to see what I had accomplished. He loved construction.

We now own a beautiful modern warehouse with seismic racking that reaches as high as twenty-seven feet, complete with many pickers, forklifts, and all the necessary equipment.

This new warehouse and office space was built with the intentions of it lasting ten years. It wasn't even our third year when we realized that we had outgrown the facility again. By then, we had inventoried enough to supply a hundred stores, not just our small group of franchisees. The question was, what were we to do? We tried to buy the 50,000-square-feet building behind us, easy enough for the forklift and the equipment to drive across the parking lot delivering product between the buildings, but the owner didn't want to sell. So we leased an additional 25,000-square-feet next door.

Business was good; we were continually opening new franchise locations across the country. The growth of the warehouse gave us the money to hire the much-needed staff and purchase the required warehouse equipment. Up until then, we had always purchased used forklifts and old picker trucks that forever broke down; but now we could afford to buy new and many more pieces of the best in equipment. The warehouse is clean, efficient, has a large backup generator, and operates on a massive computer and bar code system.

It's geared to run lean and mean because of the cost plus margins we operate on.

Our corporate offices are located at the front of the facility, along with our education centre and the realistic mock up retail store for training and seminars.

Trade shows would now have to be held outside the warehouse because of lack of space. By now, we had grown and opened many more stores; attendance would easily hit 150 people, including manufacturer representatives. We chose the Bayshore Inn in downtown Vancouver. They loved having Cap-it at the convention facility. We would always bring several custom-accessorized jeeps and pickup trucks and placed them inside the convention facility and out at the front entrance. It created an excitement they hadn't seen before. We were always welcome there.

At that time we had have three franchisee meetings a year, a supplier trade show and dinner cruise, business intelligence seminar, and fall training convention.

11 Quite a Ride

It was 1995 and I thought we had found exactly what we needed. A large American company wanted to have the master rights to our franchise in eastern USA. They wanted all the territory from the Mississippi east. Wow, this was just what we were looking for. The entrepreneur that I am, was always asking for the, "what ifs", what if a large company saw our franchise concept, liked what we had created and wanted to help us take this concept across the country. Wouldn't that be great! Somehow, I always knew that we would have many stores across the country, I just didn't know when and how long it would take. I thought this applicant would just be the thing we needed.

It was at a time in our slow growth period that I thought we had finally found a faster way to grow the company. This American applicant, Bob was part of a very large organization in the USA. They owned many auto dealerships. They were financially very well off and being in the auto industry wanted to take our franchise concept across the eastern USA. Bob was absolutely intrigued with our concept. He had never seen anything like it before. It was a WOW for us. I especially thought this would be our ticket to a faster expansion which we so desperately needed. It turned out that we just learned a big lesson, but upon reflection, a lesson I don't regret learning.

We had just placed an ad in the Canadian National Franchise magazine that was distributed across North America when we got the call. The man spoke softly at first, asking questions, and then boldly told me that he wanted to buy a Cap-it franchise, and that he wanted to bring it to his city in the eastern United States. Sort of faraway,

I thought. Like many other telephone conversations I had, I took it in stride, knowing that it would probably go nowhere. I couldn't tell from his voice or his style of questioning if he was actually a candidate that I would consider. To preserve his anonymity, I will refer to him as Bob.

Bob called us every day and sixty- to ninety-minute conversations were not uncommon; however, I did dread taking his calls in the evening, although I often did. He insisted that my partner and I fly out to see him and demonstrate our franchise to him. We would have to come up with an ingenious plan to see if he was for real. We asked for a non-refundable deposit of $5,000 in US funds, enough to pay for our flights and our time. If he accepted, and provided a personal financial statement, we would make the trip.

We finally got his financial statement. This guy could buy us out many, many times over. What did he want with a small company like ours? They were out of our league; they could do the franchise without us. Who were these guys?

We flew first-class and were greeted by a well-dressed driver. Anyone who knows my partner, Bilon, knows that he dresses casually. Running shoes and a shirt that's never tucked is everyday wear. I tried to prepare him for a dressier appearance. We might as well make a good impression, I thought. After all, they're paying to be entertained, so let's give them their money's worth.

We were taken to one of their auto dealerships, and waited in the small showroom to meet Bob. Bilon, being a former GMC dealer, was surprised to see a Dodge Viper on display in a Cadillac showroom, along with a Ford Mustang. When he finally came, the introduction was quick and to the point as if to say, Time's wasting. Bob was a short, intense, suntanned individual and was never without an entourage. He said, "Follow me, gentlemen, I want to show you our business."

It had now been at least ninety minutes since we left the airport—certainly enough time to have made our first evaluations. Bob and his men were all business, and it looked as though they had connections at General Motors. Who else would have a competitor's car in a GM showroom? This wouldn't hurt, I thought! As we followed the group outside, we heard an intense earthshaking vibration, and a Jet Ranger helicopter landed between the parked cars on the sales lot, inches away from the front entrance. Bob wanted to show off his company. We boarded the helicopter.

Nothing in my life could have prepared me for what was about to happen. Sometimes, when I think back on all this, I truly believe that the experience that day was worth it all. Had all the years of pushing the envelope brought me to this point in my life? Some very wealthy person wanted to get my approval. It was the ride of my life. We strapped on our radio-controlled helmets and began our ascent toward the skyline, adrenaline still pouring into our veins. We hovered over the city. No one can get a permit to fly into a parking lot in the middle of a city. Again, I thought, who are these guys? The thought that crossed my mind during the trip was: wouldn't it be great if these guys actually helped us open stores in the USA!

As we were told later by one of his aides, Bob does not carry a driver's license, because if he was ever stopped, once a policeman realized who he was, they had to let him go. He had a VIP reputation in his town.

We flew to several of his dealerships, landing on their sales lots. Bob explained that he owned many large businesses throughout America. If a situation arose and we could not land close to one of his businesses, he had a chauffeur with a Lincoln or a Cadillac waiting, ready to take us wherever. As the day progressed, little talk about Cap-it or our system took place. His time was spent trying to impress the two of us. We were quite impressed, to say the least, until we flew to his private hangar.

Have you ever seen a white floor shine as brightly as the glistening snow? We did, it was the floor of the hangar that housed eight of his personal jets. One large jet was dedicated to flying the local city's football team to their games. We were now way, way beyond being impressed.

That evening, we went out to dinner at his private golf club. Bob could never remember what he ordered for dinner that night, or any other night; nor could he tell you what he just ate. Someone would have to remind him. His energy was spent, as he put it, "on more important things." His left-brain psyche disabled him when it came to opening a door with a key. After fumbling and dropping the keys several times, I asked if I could help. He always needed help.

Despite sleeping only three to four hours a night, Bob was supremely focused. He was fun to be with, but usually in another world, trying to stay ahead of the conversation. Often you saw him whispering into the ears of others passing by, leaving us wondering what all these hidden conversations were all about.

After dinner, he suggested watching the video commercial that I had brought along. His aides attempted, without luck, to find a VCR that was working in the clubhouse. "Never mind," he said. "Follow me." So into the cars we filed. Lots of muttering and laughter later, we ended up in someone's driveway.

Since he did not even know the owner of this very posh house, Bob spoke to the young man who was house-sitting and asked him if he could use the TV and video machine for a few minutes. You have got to be kidding! I thought. Just being with this guy was an experience most people would never have. The young man let us in after another whispered conversation took place. There were seven of us.

Bob would never take no for an answer. He told me some time later, when I questioned him regarding his boldness, that he once made a bet with a university friend. He said that he could get the pope in the Vatican on the telephone line to speak with him.

"How did you do that, Bob?" I asked.

"It was simple," he said. "All I did was impress upon the man answering that it was a life-and-death situation, and that I was a dying man, begging and pleading. I only had hours to live, and that I needed to speak personally to Pope John Paul." And it happened!

I know for a fact that it could happen. That's how he got in touch with me one day when I was out dining at a restaurant and I thought no one knew where I was. Well, Bob found me. He had called long-distance to everyone who was ever connected to me and finally tracked me down.

During this time, we signed the franchise agreement and proceeded to set up two stores, with vast plans to set up ten to twenty more within the next year or two.

It was an exciting time knowing that we were opening stores in the USA. At that time, I also worked as operations manager and had to take many lengthy trips to the stores, either setting up showrooms and or for training. I remember a midnight flight that I took to do another training session when I got lost on one of their eight lane freeways. It was twelve midnight, pitch black and no street lights. I had driven at least thirty miles past the exit; so I thought, or maybe I was on the wrong freeway, I couldn't tell. I was lost. I pulled the rental car over and stopped at the side of the road. A little frightened, I asked myself, "what am I doing here in the middle of nowhere?". What had I got myself into? Was I pushing myself too hard for the sake of my dream? Was it worth endangering myself?

And out of nowhere, while looking at the map, I heard a knock on my driver's side window, scaring me half to death. Luckily it was the highway patrol, a very pleasant officer. He asked if I needed help and offered to take me directly to the town and hotel that I was to stay for the night. I couldn't help but think, someone was watching over me.

Despite the difficulties of having stores on the other side of the continent and the long flights, it was a good time for me. However, we found that the distance had created a disconnect with the franchisee and the staff. Because of the great distance we made the decision to do the initial training on site rather than insisting they fly their managers to our facilities. It was a mistake, we should have insisted that their team fly out to our offices first and see how we do business. Another lesson we learned.

Bob was letting someone else run the division, someone who had other priorities, and that meant Cap-it would have to go. The day I got the news, I felt that an era had ended. Someone was taking care of us, and I knew it would be for the best.

I have experienced what few people have. I was there, I saw it, I felt it, and I have to say that the pleasures along the way would be an understatement. We all enjoyed ourselves. It was an adrenaline rush being with Bob.

Coming from a small town in British Columbia and being exposed to Bob and his people, allowed me to experience people with power and great wealth, people you only talk about but never experience. As much as I like money, I had chosen my family as number one on my list of priorities. The total experience had confirmed that having to shut down the two stores was better overall. Bob and his people were extremely good at business and making money. As for having stores in the USA, I knew something else would come along later.

12 Dinner Cruise

Dressed for the dry August evening, we walked along the harborside, smiling at the unique names given to the different yachts. The dinner cruise was just about to begin, and soft and excited laughter echoed as we walked aboard. It was Cap-it's annual convention; over one hundred attending franchisees and suppliers were going to have an evening to remember.

Our destination was up Indian Arm to a small Haida village, about two hours of slow casual cruising up the inlet.

Breathless and amazed, we held our drinks while gathering at the stern of the yacht. Across the inlet, you could see the still reflection of North Vancouver and its mountains reaching into Coal Harbour. Magic was in the air. It transcended the horizon as we beheld the city of Vancouver at its finest. Could there be an evening any finer than this?

An entertainer by nature, my mind drifted back to my first experience in Disneyland. That's the feeling I always want to give the people around me. Romance them into another world, create the fantasy that we all crave in our hearts, and take them far away from their everyday troubles.

Giving our franchisees the very best there was to offer that night paralleled the service I planned to give them. There wasn't a person there that evening who doubted if they had bought the right franchise. Evenings like this created the energy and positive atmosphere we all needed; and because of that and everyone's approval, we've continued the dinner cruise each year.

Anyone who runs a franchise knows that the best day of a franchisee's life is the day they begin. Nothing has gone wrong, and everything looks great. It's the high expectation and what the business will do for them that create problems later on. We categorize most franchise businesses as "no-brainers." However, it did take a brain to run our franchise. Unlike others, we are a specialty store, and we sell knowledge.

We had made a lot of mistakes in the first few years—choosing the wrong people in the beginning were some of the mistakes—but tonight we were going to have a good time. This night would be as good as it got. When I look back on this weekend, I see time well spent, but mainly a special time in my life where my wife and I were proud of what we had accomplished. Life can be quite a ride if we only get up and do something. And we did just that.

In my dreams, we would take people to new heights in business and in their personal lives. I love to motivate, and I love to sell dreams. I'm a salesman. I'm always selling: it may be the restaurant where we had great food, it may be the new jeans that I just bought, or it may be the lifestyle I live. I'm forever trying to convince people of a better idea. It was my intention to build a better life for the struggling independent.

> *Keeping ourselves focused on our goals forces nature to surrender its secrets. The problem is that there may be trade-offs we are not willing to accept. After all, we may have to forsake friends and family to achieve some discoveries.*

I remember the story of Thomas Edison and his response when asked, "Where did you find the answers to your discoveries?"

"It was nature itself that explained the mystery to me," he would reply.

He would lie on the grass with his eyes to the skies, listening to nature. Keeping ourselves focused on our goals forces nature to surrender its secrets. The problem is that there may be trade-offs we are not willing to accept. After all, we may have to forsake friends and family to achieve some discoveries.

Throughout life, I kept seeing that the journey toward my dream might very well be the reward itself. Meeting difficulties, experiencing characters from all walks of life, giving up the things that I once held sacred, compromising on important issues, fighting fear, and so on—all contributed to the quality of the ride.

13 The Questioning Years

What Could I Say
1991

It was well into the morning when my receptionist asked me if I had time to meet an acquaintance that just happened to drop by for a visit. He was a well-respected member of the community. I know him by name, but I'd rather not mention it. I invited him in to my office, and we visited. As always, he was well dressed, wearing a suit and tie, very professional and polite. He was extremely interested in what we were doing. And so I went on to tell him about our plans. Franchising seemed to captivate his mind. He asked me questions about how things were going, and we spoke of our newly formed franchise. As we talked, he shared his concern regarding our goal of opening many truck accessory stores throughout the province. I didn't know if he was envious of us or what he was up to.

We continued to talk for about an hour. Frankly, I was impressed that such a man would take the time to pay me a visit. He was much older, and I knew he was very knowledgeable and experienced in the world of business. Strange thing was, he began to talk about all the bad things that could happen to me and the company if I continued on this course. At first I thought this guy was definitely jealous but I had the time and decided to hear him out. He said he had seen this kind of business venture before, and in most cases, it didn't end well for the friends that he knew. He began to warn me of the pitfalls that lay ahead and the consequences of such a risky venture. The more we talked, the more he expanded on what he really wanted to say. From what I saw, he came to visit and to warn me of the dangers that lay ahead. He gave examples of friends of his that did much the same in franchising and experienced terrific hurdles and unforeseen problems that overwhelmed the owners to the point that some of them actually took their own lives. He said one of them actually jumped off a bridge.

What could I say? He came into my office at a time when we were full of great expectations and hope for the future. No one could put a damper on our plans. I knew what I wanted and where I was going. As great a man as I thought he was, he was just another flake that I had to put up with. No one was going to rain on my parade. Like I said in the beginning, I was young and naïve and full of dreams. This could never apply to me. I forgot about the visit and went on my way. Things were going really well: newspaper articles were written about us saying that we were one of the fastest-growing franchises in Vancouver. 1991 was a fantastic year.

A few months earlier, the president of a major manufacturer of truck caps also came to see me, in the same office, and told me that the word going around in the industry was that "the demise of Cap-it is imminent."

What do you do with stuff like that? I was looking for validation, not condemnation. It didn't feel good, to say the least. It was this comment that hurt me more than ever, because he was in the same industry as I was. Were they all jealous, or did they know something that I didn't know? I thought people could see and read the future as I saw it, and that franchising a fragmented industry was only natural. Someone had to do it, and I saw myself as the one to do so. This guy traveled 500 miles to tell me this; go figure? Was I a threat? I wasn't planning on competing with him in manufacturing, what was his problem? The best I can say is that envy must have played a role. However, the prophecy of the dangers that lay ahead of me I ignored totally.

It's been many years since that day, but I can tell you, everything that man forewarned came true: I experienced it all, every pitfall, the unrelenting pain, and everything that could possibly go wrong went wrong, except for one thing. I never considered jumping off a bridge and taking my own life, but I can see why others did. I was driven to that point, but somehow I escaped.

When I think about that time long ago, I ask myself, did he come to warn me? Was I supposed to take heed and cancel my dream because of fear? Maybe I was like little David with a slingshot, determined to slay Goliath. I must have had the faith that he had. I could do it, just like David. I, too, was fearless, at the time.

***

A Few Years Later,

Those tough years in business, questioning why bad things were happening, made me sit up and take a look at myself. Had I done anything to attract the calamities of events we encountered during the last seven years? Where did I go wrong? Every day appeared to bring its own set of disasters, and just when you thought that it couldn't get any worse, it did. Now, with little money to pay the bills and someone starting legal action against me, everything teetered on the brink. My integrity was at stake. Nothing more fearful could have ripped through me than losing my reputation, especially at this low point. I felt forsaken. I had never been sued for not meeting my obligations. I remember saying, "I wouldn't wish these difficulties upon anyone." The pain we experienced during those years was like a trip through hell. I remember the one-hour drives to and from our office, and how I used to curse at all the things that had taken place that day. This went on for years. Nothing seemed to be working right. Each time I would begin a new strategy, it would fail, with devastating results. I poured more and more of my money into the company until nothing was left.

It was 1992, one year after we began franchising, that this legal action, started. It really got my attention. An individual claimed that we misrepresented our services and that I was now held responsible. It was odd but difficult to understand. I had been in business for fifteen years by then, and I never had a customer that I couldn't satisfy. Customer frustration is always part of business and individuals can make unrealistic claims but we always found ways to solve the problem and satisfy the individual and keep them happy. We never even came close to going to court. However, this legal action shook me up, I could not believe it was happening. It appeared that no conversation could solve this. The individual was just adamant that I pay for damages. The other reason it shook me up was that no one was working harder at servicing than I was.

The lawsuit never went to court, and it turned out that all the individual ever wanted was to not pay their account, which was in the tens of thousands of dollars for inventory purchased. A lot of money at that time. We lost that money. The issue was that it took several years of waiting to finally end. That individual carried on in business for a while until one of them got arrested and imprisoned for a different issue.

It didn't take us long to figure out that not everyone had the same work business acumen or work ethic and desire to succeed as I had. Another lesson we learned was to choose franchise applicants carefully, although finance is extremely important, personality and skill set is equally important. In the early days, we had chosen some applicants who did not have the skill set to manage and or follow a system. Lesson number one, we improved the criteria in selecting and approving franchise applicants and found out that we needed to spend more time training and monitoring their performance. All this took time to learn and at great cost and pain.

Next, we lost our flagship product line (the Bac-Pac Truck Cap) because of their inferior manufacturing process; on top of that, hundreds of frustrated customers wanted their money back. In addition to all that, two of our stores had to be resold due to mismanagement. While some mismanaged their affairs and wanted out, others were either getting divorced or struck down with serious illnesses. During this time, some of the stores were not paying their bills, and our suppliers demanded we make good on all monies owed.

A few years later, I was forced to take on partners in an effort to survive. I eventually traded my controlling shares of the company for the survival and benefit of the entire organization. I was now accountable to partners. I was forced to cut my salary, sell our second car, sell our dream home, give up our retirement savings toward company losses and to reinvest in further infrastructure; and by this time, we still owed more than we owned.

The philosophy that kept me going

This once-inspired dream of mine had turned into a curse. The plan was that everyone should benefit. "Tackle something so big that it is bound to fail if a Higher Power is not in it" was the underlying energy. Why do you think I'm writing this book? I saw so much suffering, and all I could do was sit by and watch.

If you visit my library, you will see just about every book and autobiography on business and philosophy. Some books tell of their successes, some of their good timing, but most of them tell of their good fortune. I was not too proud to learn from others. From the beginning, my quest for wisdom had led me to

> *"Tackle something so big that it is bound to fail if a Higher Power is not in it"*

search the world over for the secrets of success. If it meant reading hundreds of books and networking with as many individuals as I could, I would do it.

Searching for clues led me to take a year off to study Christian philosophy at the Canadian Bible Institute. Reading philosophy from Soren Kierkegaard, St. Augustine's *Confessions*, John Bunyan, C. S. Lewis and his *Screwtape Letters* all brought me to a heightened understanding of people. It was comforting to know that many others had encountered difficulties like I had.

Anger set in. There are many biblical verses that appear to romance your dreams. "Ask anything in my name, and I will give it."

"Ask and you shall receive."

"You have not because you ask not."

And then the prayer of Jabez: "Bless my works and increase my lands," "plants a seed of faith," and "I will pour down such a blessing, pressed down in full measure that one cannot hold."

Not one of these things made sense. Were they riddles for us to solve, or were they wishful ideas written by men? They're all conditional, some say. "Man has his plan, and God has his plan, and man's plan doesn't matter." That became my understanding. What would you have done?

I was in business, contractually responsible for others, and I needed to help them. It was even more difficult, knowing that close business acquaintances of mine were experiencing exponential growth and success year after year in their business. What could I do to help the people who were counting on me?

I have many memories of Elaine putting in many long hours in those years, doing all the bookkeeping for all our companies and trying to keep up with the workload. Looking back, it was all work then and no play. We would quit work after an eight-to-ten-hour day and go home for the second shift. We just couldn't get business out of our mind.

In 2001, her dad died. Two weeks later, her brother also passed away; and in between the two funerals, Mason got married. Funny how life works! Elaine had a very difficult time; she had lost half her family in two weeks. Her parents only had the two children, and now it would be just her mom and herself. Six months prior to this my Dad had also passed away.

I remember calling my contact at KPMG and asking him for help with the bookkeeping and accounting. Elaine couldn't focus and she needed help.

Tending to family matters while working

My mother became ill and depressed after Dad passed away. Eventually, her depression became chronic. She would not let it go or accept the new life without Dad. Two years had passed, and with no further progress, she continued to cry every day. She was blessed with sixty-two years of marriage, five children, and seventeen great-grand-children. She had been given a wonderful life. When I asked her to reflect on a life full of blessings, she continued to lament about what she had lost. She said she had nothing to live for anymore.

What do you tell a person that has nothing to live for? It's like someone programming them selves to die. Despite my efforts, she continued her martyr's pilgrimage to nowhere. It was then that the *power thought* came to me. Again, out of adversity and uncertainties, I found an answer. "Why don't you live for the pride of accomplishment—pride in yourself, pride of enduring, fighting and finishing the race that life gave you? Show the Creator that you can bear it, if only for a few days, in repayment for all the goodness he has shown you in your eighty years?"

Maybe I was too harsh on the old lady. Anyway, if not for her, it was for me. After that day, I understood one thing: the Creator knew her struggle just like he knew mine. When you begin to realize that the Creator is aware of your sufferings, you don't feel alone anymore. You begin to take on the stalwart approach and feed off of the once-negative forces.

It was then that I realized I could feed off of the uncertainties. Each day became a new adventure for me. Looking back, I saw how every major unforeseen circum-

> *"Why don't you live for the pride of accomplishment—pride in yourself, pride of enduring, fighting and finishing the race that life gave you? Show the Creator that you can bear it, if only for a few days, in repayment for all the goodness he has shown you in your eighty years?"*

stance had shaped my life. And I also saw how these uncertainties were controlling my destiny. Had my mother grasped this concept, she could have, if nothing else, experienced relief from her despair.

The willingness to accept the unknown and understand the wisdom of uncertainties creates freedom from fear and freedom from the past. When we accept life's uncertainties, we become connected to everything and we become the Creator's infinite possibility.

Less Is More

In 1987, my business was an unpredictable place that kept me always prepared, honed in to the keen edge of life. Still focused on my goal but giving myself little opportunity to sit back and relax, I forged ahead. It's common knowledge that a business has to grow. If you are standing still, you ultimately go backward. It was this philosophy that kept me from taking the much-needed slower approach to business. My strong will to achieve had bought me my first Mercedes and now had already given me a newer one just two years later. I was in my early forties.

> *The willingness to accept the unknown and understand the wisdom of uncertainties creates freedom from fear and freedom from the past. When we accept life's uncertainties, we become connected to everything and we become the Creator's infinite possibility.*

I felt the total weight of my responsibility. The vise was closing in on me, and I didn't like the grip it appeared to have. People were depending on me, and I didn't have enough cash to pay the bills. "I've been here so many times before," taking three steps ahead and then having to take two backward. Was it all worth it? Why did I spend so much time attaining when the price for growth would sometimes become unbearable? I had to find a way to build the business without always placing my finances in jeopardy.

The "bigger is better" life was beginning to show its self-centered ideology. Masking its purely selfish motive to a belief that striving for perfection is the worthy goal has its limitations. So there is no safe place; even your philosophy will eventually let you down. And so I began to find great meaning in living with the understanding that less is more.

Trying to find a deal or see if I could do without became as much fun as spending. Comparing prices at the grocery store was a highlight. Even though I had the finances to ignore prices, I made a point of looking for good value in everything I did.

My Brother-In-Law

My brother-in-law born in 1933, now eighty years old, still remembers the time as a young boy in Russia, asking his mom if there would ever come a time in his life when he could eat all the buns he ever wanted. You had to be there to understand it. Very seldom will a dinner go by that he doesn't recall the memory of that time in his life, and with a tiny tear, he tells the story. His dad was taken from the family by the Russians when he was four years old. Growing up, he felt the responsibility of taking care of his mother. I have always been appreciative of his story and the influence he has had through friends and our family.

14 No Back Door

The energy that fueled my desire to franchise came from the hunger of wanting to achieve.

"It's better to have tried something big and failed than never to have tried anything and succeeded." Positive proverbs like this continued to flash before my mind as if there were no other words that had more significance or purpose in my life. When I heard one, it would plant itself within my brain for later use. The insatiable thirst for a fuller and more meaningful life consumed me each day.

As a child, I grew up with a strong faith and was taught that faith brought rewards to those who trusted. I would make certain to do my part. However, the disappointments and uncertainties that came through the years soon gave way to doubt. The bitterness and resentment, at times, fueled my anger and made me rethink my youthful philosophy. Low self-esteem gave way to a lack of confidence: would I fail, or would I prove them wrong?

My father had the best intentions as he raised his children and did the best he knew how. However, I took the position that I *was* neglected. Left to fend for myself, in most cases; and while he was busily trying to survive himself, I learned to take care of myself. He had grown up in an environment where the younger generation got little attention or respect. Children were just too young to understand adult concepts. In today's world, small children appear to take on the role of advisors, the opposite of my father's time. I eventually thanked my father for all the things he didn't do for me and became proud that I had become a survivor just like him. All was eventually forgiven the day he replied, "I did the best I knew how." And I truly understood his intentions for me. What I thought were his short-comings in his life became my advantage; it was his way of teaching me to stay alive. I became like him, a survivor.

Like many other families, each child, I'm sure, had feelings of being misunderstood. There were five of us in the family—three sisters and a brother. I was the fourth child. My brother, the oldest, nine years ahead of me, continued to set the perfect example. I was to emulate him in all my tasks, my mother thought. "Why can't you be like your brother?" He was kind, soft-spoken, thoughtful, and diligent in all his chores. I would take the role of the black sheep, and why not? It would balance the family; you can't have five perfect kids.

Although my fantasies of wealth and prosperity took a back seat to my parents' daily struggles, as a child, I silently pursued my dreams whenever I could. And when I eventually moved out of the house and got married, there would be no looking back. I was now free to pursue my choices.

The Partnership

In my mind, a commitment was just that—a commitment. It was a dedication to a plan someone believed in. I found out later that commitments usually have no back doors or exit routes. Years later, I would realize that I had not planned an escape route; failure was just not in the equation at that point in my life. The inescapable force of wanting to achieve pressed me even farther to the mark of no return; and the

> *commitments usually have no back doors or exit routes*

thought of failure had not even crossed my mind. Some would call this faith, and some would call it naivete. Whether in ignorance or not, I did learn about the price of a commitment.

As young children, we can make major changes along the way with little consequences; but as adults, our decisions generally become irreversible, at least very difficult to change. Adults make commitments and see them through, knowing the great costs attendant to that commitment. The marriage, the mortgage, the kids, and the career usually come first, and that's when we learn what a commitment is all about. We don't have any back-door plans for these. We blindly move ahead, blissfully anticipating a better life.

It was this approach that brought me to a dream that would not be easy to achieve. With nowhere to run and nowhere to hide, I persevered. The journey brought me to a greater understanding of others who had gone before me, making sacrifices and learning to cope with failure. Venturing ahead knowing that the only back door I had if it didn't work out was just more hard work.

Taking on partners in an effort to survive opened our minds even further; it was a time of learning. My partners' approach was different than mine. They focused strictly on profits, and relationships had little to do with business in their mind. People had always been our greatest asset, and never to be taken for granted. Relationships were a priority in my mind. It had worked for them, and no matter what I said, I could not change that. And in a way, they were right: a company is valued according to the profit it generates, no matter how good it treats its people or its suppliers.

At that time, all we had was potential. The years of my sacrifice and financial investment in the hundreds of thousands of dollars meant very little to our new partners. It was a humiliating experience, but nevertheless a move I was forced to make to survive. They came in like bulldozers. Changes were made; they threw out anything that appeared foreign and everything I held sacred. Their plan was to direct the company into a spurt of real growth. Despite their efforts, it never happened.

I had started the company primarily selling truck canopies, but as the years passed, we had to add truck accessories to our mix. In order to stay profitable, we had to expand our product base. Truck accessories were the logical choice. A customer coming to our store for a canopy would be an easy sale for added accessories. It worked well, and the demand grew steadily, to the point that new designs and accessories fueled the constant demand. In the beginning, 85%

of our sales came from truck caps; today caps run at approximately 23%. Accessories and covers make up the balance.

We ran into a problem with the truck accessory side of it. We were buying the truck caps direct from the manufacturer; however, the truck accessories were purchased through a local wholesale distributor, who was making the normal 33% margin. The problem was that everyone else was purchasing from the distributor as well, so there was no advantage for us. A franchise should give the franchisee an edge, and we knew it. So we crafted a strategic alliance with Lyco. It didn't work. They kept threatening us by selling to our competitors; they reasoned that they needed to move more product. We had to find another way.

Along came the Alberta Truck Outfitters—owners and partners Andrew Bilon, Jim White, and Fred Fishburne. We had seen the power of owning your own warehouse through them and what it could do. The Outfitters had a warehouse that served their seven retail locations in Alberta. They were profitable, and they were able to sell at discounted pricing and still make great margins. I wanted to do the same for our stores. We wanted to bypass the middleman and buy directly from manufacturers.

After many months of strategic thinking and planning, I knew I had to partner with them in an effort to save our franchise. By this time it appeared we had no choice, I needed to save the franchise and get better pricing. The price I would have to pay for this partnership would be insurmountable. It would be a deal with no back door for me. The Outfitters ended up with a majority share position—60% of Cap-it—and in return, Cap-it was able to purchase from the Outfitters warehouse at cost plus pricing. The plan and promise for me was that I'd have a smaller piece of a bigger pie. Our stores, combined with their stores, would make us the largest chain in Canada. The 50/50 partnership deal that I wanted didn't work for Bilon. He wanted the additional extra controlling share for his influence, or the edge he felt he needed to keep his partners on board. And I felt I had no other choice. Bilon did not have controlling shares in the Outfitters, and it was his way of keeping the partners in check. I have to admire Bilon for one thing—and that was that he did give me his word that if the day came, he would sell me back the controlling share portion of 10%. The smaller piece of a bigger pie sounded reasonable, especially when I considered the extra revenue Cap-it would receive from Alberta's seven store royalties.

Before any of this could take place, I had to talk to my minority shareholder, Bill Fast. I told him that I didn't think we had any choice. I went on to explain that we'd have a smaller piece of a bigger pie. Bill had come in as partner two years after we started the company. He was a very faithful and trusting man. We needed his cash investment to finance the intense legal work to pass the Alberta Disclosure Act and get provincial approval to franchise in Alberta. Plus, we had other financing issues that needed cash desperately. Bill agreed to the new partnership, and we moved forward.

We officially began the partnership. Together we were now the largest chain of truck accessory stores in Canada, totaling 14 stores. Initially, there was a sense of relief. It was good for the franchisees, but not that good for me. The dream I had from the beginning became a nightmare. We now had four people running the Cap-it franchise, and each one had different ideas. Each one had egos the size of buses. Granted, my new partners knew how to make money—but at what cost, was the question. The contracts were signed, and shortly afterward, the difficulties began.

I remained president and founder of Cap-it; my salary remained the same. It was in those years that I realized I had run my business with respect and not fear. My partners had a very different style of management. I saw how fear and intimidation worked, and it worked well; but it just wasn't my style. I had learned that perceived value was the foundational approach to building a better franchise. It's how the franchisees *perceive things* that really matter. Making them feel a part of a great organization was important to me. Franchisees can have great ideas. Owning your own stores is a different matter; the owner remains virtually a dictator, where fear can work well. My partners owned their own stores in Alberta. However, I believe that managing by respect is a much better way of running a franchise. I know that franchisors always say that franchisees think that "if it succeeds, they have done it, and if it fails, I've done it." And this is where the two philosophies of the partnership collided. Bilon saw my side, but the others did not.

A year later, we realized that we needed a cash injection. Bilon and his partners never did inject cash into the company when they received their initial shares. The company now needed cash to move forward. The original deal was, I would have to give up shares in the company for the ability to purchase from their warehouse in Alberta on a cost-plus basis. This became the trade off. Yes, I know what you're thinking and that's exactly what I thought at the time. However, the ability to buy all our truck accessories on a cost-plus was paramount for the success of the franchisees and I knew it. Without this buying power, Cap-it would have failed and I wasn't willing to accept that fate.

Bilon and his partners showed me the financials statements of their seven Alberta stores before the deal was made and proved that they were extremely profitable. They had figured out that a warehouse could save them lots money and give them the profits they needed. This was what I wanted for our franchisees. As bitter as it was, I felt the trade off was the price I would pay to keep Cap-it going.

Bilon and his Alberta partners had now been with Cap-it for about a year when we realized that we needed more than just a warehouse to buy at discounted prices. Again, I learned, it's never one thing, it always takes many things to bring a plan together.

Bilon and I would spend countless hours strategizing how to improve the growth of Cap-it. Time and time again we would spend long evenings at the restaurant with a glass of wine or two discussing different ideas, trying to come up with a plan. Most of our ideas would take time and money.

Bilon quickly realized that franchisees were much different than the men he had hired to manage his own stores. We had to use an approach that took the role of a coach rather than that of a dictator/ boss.

One plan we came up with was to allow the stores to purchase directly from our manufacturers, saving the franchisees even more money than buying from the Alberta warehouse. The plan went forward. We would allow stores to purchase some product directly from the manufacturers, as long as they met the minimum prepaid freight allowance. Meaning that they would get free shipping if they purchased in quantity and met the dollar figure for free shipping. Our head office charged a minimal fee for this.

The problem we encountered was that some of the franchisees did not pay their invoices on time, forcing the supplier to cut off credit to everyone at Cap-it. This included the Alberta warehouse as well. It was just awful, so we came up with a plan to guarantee all account and payments. There was no way that we would allow Cap-it's credit rating to be other than perfect.

It was not an easy road for Bilon and myself. The dream of building a better franchise continued to consume us. We would come to the office each morning, solve problems and then try to create yet another plan to improve the system. It had worked for Bilon and his partners in Alberta. Why wasn't it working here? The Alberta Truck Outfitters had been hugely profitable with their stores. We asked ourselves, why was it so difficult with the Cap-it stores.

We had several franchisees at the time that were doing well financially and understood the new systems we had put in place. But some franchisees could not catch on to the changes and that required us to hire additional staff to monitor stores management abilities. An operations manager was hired and operations instructor to educate, observe and check progress of the stores performance.

Keith Peron was a friend of Bilon. He had just sold a very large and successful company in Vancouver and wanted to come in as a partner. He saw the potential of being involved in a franchise like ours. Keith was excited to lend his expertise to the organization and was willing to inject some badly needed cash. A deal was struck and agreed to, including the decision to have Keith's wife come in as our new head office accountant.

Elaine had to be removed from her day to day duties to make room for Keith's wife. Up until now the accounting for head office was being done in our Surrey corporate store. Elaine, along with some part time staff, managed both the Corporate accounting and Surrey retail store bookkeeping. Keith's proposal was that his wife join us as a hired accountant. I wasn't used to being without Elaine beside me. Especially when I was quizzed about accounting matters or filing from prior days. It was very difficult for Elaine, to be always be ready to answer a telephone call regarding some question Keith's wife had. It was a bitter/sweet decision for both of us.

Bringing in another partner meant that our existing share position would change again and be reduced even further. The considerable amount of cash he was injecting would compensate for this. This, of course, took my minority share position down to 28% but I still remained president. His active role would now take us to the level that we were so much looking forward to.

The sad part was that I had to go back to Bill and explain that if we accepted Keith as partner his minority share would be cut back again, just like mine. This would be the third time I'd go to Bill and give him the good news and bad news storey. Bill initially came in as minority partner with me, but when Bilon came in as partner, Bill's shares were almost cut in half. Now with Keith coming in, all our shares would be cut back one more time.

The partners must have felt that my team couldn't make it work so they were willing to try something new. To say it was a bad time for Elaine and I would be an understatement. We both endured much pain and humiliation. As difficult as it was, I had made all these decisions to benefit the stores. I couldn't let them down no matter what the price.

Keith's strategy was customer care, which we all rallied behind. He had always considered this top priority and I believed it served him well in his former business. However, a year or two later, nothing had changed, and we bought him out. Customer care is important but it was not the only thing we needed to bring the company to greater success.

Andrew Bilon had now moved to Vancouver from his office in Edmonton. Why we located our new office in Burnaby, an hour's travel time from home, I still don't know. We were trying anything and everything we could to make a difference. I remember traveling to the Burnaby office across the dreaded Port Mann Bridge in the mornings while my wife and our two boys drove to the Surrey store. For an escape during the day, I would drive to the Surrey store and visit the family and staff that were always loyal to me. Then maybe in the afternoon, I would drive to our Langley store to see what was happening. We had opened the corporate store in Langley a half hour from Surrey. My job was to keep an eye on Surrey and Langley while working in Burnaby.

Andrew Bilon and the partners had shares in Cap-it International, but during this time, I still owned 100% of the Surrey and Langley stores, plus a very small warehouse we named Western Warehouse in Surrey. Now working in Vancouver, Bilon helped me establish contact with American manufacturers and suppliers and built up our distribution base in our small warehouse. It worked this time. Manufacturers and their reps were reluctant at first, but when they found out that we wanted to establish a BC warehouse, and that we were leaving the Alberta warehouse, they supported us.

At that time, the industry was unwilling to open more warehouse distribution; they felt it was oversaturated. I can see why even today there are too many small companies buying direct. They must purchase in large quantities, and when they can't move the product fast enough, they are forced to clear it out and sell at cost. That's where price cutting comes in. It's a tricky thing. Independents always look for the lowest price and then without realizing it, they sell it at a reduced price. So in the end, their margins are much less than at a Cap-it store.

The original deal was that Cap-it would be buying from the Alberta warehouse at cost plus pricing. I remember a year or two earlier paying the ultimate price for that to occur, to the point that

I gave up controlling shares of Cap-it to make it happen. But I guess it was not meant to be. Bilon's partners in Alberta constantly resisted the partnership; and I knew that things could not continue the way we were going. Luckily, with Bilon's help we had already started our own warehouse in Surrey BC. The warehouse had now become a big part of the franchise system, giving us small but badly needed profits, enough to help us get to the next stage in the game.

The other phase in the plan was that the Outfitters stores would change their name to Cap-it and pay the normal royalty. That never happened because of infighting. Bilon and I couldn't convince the other partners to follow through with the initial promise of us all being part of the bigger pie. This became the unraveling of the partnership.

Despite Bilon and me going it alone, there were other factors that had to be worked out. First on the list was that we had to open our own warehouse and distribution centre in BC. It was almost impossible for us to have all the needed inventory at the beginning, so we allowed our stores to also buy additional products directly from the manufactures. We knew that a fully stocked warehouse could supply a hundred stores; we only had eleven at the time. We had an interesting call one day from our franchisee, an auto dealership principle who owned our store. He recognized what we were trying to do and that was to encourage stores to buy direct. He said it wasn't working for him but gave us an alternative plan. He preferred to pay us a higher price if we would carry the inventory for him in our warehouse, so he didn't have to buy in such large quantities. This would allow him to be able to buy one item at a time instead of the large prepaid shipment we were offering. It was awesome to hear; the alternate plan was brilliant. He knew what we were facing and understood what was best for the total organization. And this is how the BC warehouse began to grow.

We had finally figured it out. We would carry more core inventory and sell it on a cost-plus basis to the franchisees. This structure allowed us to cover our overhead, make a small margin but still pass on considerable saving to the stores.

In the end, it was better for our stores to purchase their product directly from our own warehouse. The product was in-stock, and they didn't have to wait the normal four weeks from the manufacturer. And in addition, the store's inventory could be kept at a minimum. Our warehouse could now supply the product daily.

The other necessary ingredient for us to survive was creativity and the ability to solve problems on the fly. If you check America's top 500 companies, you will find it is their creativity that keeps them ahead of the competition. At times, it was plain tiring coming to work solving yet another set of problems and trying to create a better way to improve systems.

By this time, four years had passed and still no significant change to the growth. We had moved our corporate offices to downtown Burnaby a suburb of Vancouver. But traveling there during rush hour and especially across the Port Mann Bridge was dreadful, the bridge that crosses the Fraser River from Abbotsford was too small for the population. Today there is a ten lane bridge. At that time there were only four lanes and traffic would back up for miles. To prevent the long rush-hour traffic jams, I would have to cross the bridge before 6:00 a.m. and head back home after 6:30 p.m. That meant I'd get up at 4:30 am, eat breakfast and be at the bridge by 6:00 am to avoid traffic, a fifteen-hour day. Working long hours and trying to solve problems all day long took its toll on me.

None of my friends ever knew that I had lost control of my company and what I had sacrificed to keep the company alive. Too embarrassed to talk about it, I continued to keep working. When I look back on those days, I must have become numb. My main concern was the commitment I'd given to the franchisees, and that Cap-it would be what I said it would be. I couldn't let them down. The franchise was to better the lives of franchisees and to be a fun and profitable retail store to run. It was a very difficult time for my wife; she felt the sting of humiliation, hard work without reward and the pressure we both put on ourselves to survive that included many sleepless nights.

I truly believe my partners had good intentions, and that they wanted to help build this company into a chain of many stores. None of us had anyone to follow or to get ideas from. No one worldwide had built a truck accessory chain of stores that were run as a franchise; we were the first. We tried to model ourselves after the Muffler shops, restaurant chains, the fast-food chains, and the Century 21 franchise, none of which even came close to our model. It was trial and error that took us to where we are today.

15 A New Day

I remember the day very well. I was driving to work, and I parked my car in a quiet spot beside the road. I contemplated whether to carry on or give up. For an hour, I debated the merits of fighting to reap the rewards, if any, or continuing to live in defeat and humility. The one thing that became real to me as I sat there was the seriousness of the conversation. I was not leaving until I had an answer. I knew one way or the other I was going to conclude this thing once and for all. I had reached my brick wall, and there was nowhere to go.

My whole life passed before me. Would I choose to give up, or would I continue hoping that things would get better? By now, I had spent at least a year wishing that a bus would run me over in hopes that it would all end.

As I sat there mentally wrestling with the pros and cons, a quiet presence came over me and, in a soothing mental voice, told me the faint words, *"It won't always be this way."* And as a life preserver is to a drowning man, I grabbed on to those saving words of hope.

I drove away a new man. It seemed as though my thoughts had reached the Creator, and he had spoken back. I had a new hope; I had chosen to believe that things would get better.

I guess it was fear that kept me from seeing the possibilities around me. It stole my creativity that once fueled my day-to-day life and encompassed my leadership as a possibility thinker. The day came, and out of sheer desperation, I shouted, "Things won't always be this way!" And sure enough, it all changed The waters of affliction stopped flowing. It was never the same from that day forward. Good things began to happen each day.

Still stunned and somewhat bewildered, we carried on, keeping the business alive. We applied a new set of rules; we worked, believing things would change. There was no substitution for a careful and deliberate approach to business. "The devil is in the details" became our motto. By this time we were forced to sell our dream home on the mountain and move to a small condo in town. From a Corvette to a Hyundai, much money had been lost. My wife cried; it was a very difficult time for her.

The questions were still there: why had such devastation taken place in the early 1990s when our hopes and faith were always so high? Why did so many people have to suffer?

I remember one franchisee with a young family was being treated for a tumor and was forced to sell. Another newly wed couple divorced because of arguments regarding the business and had to sell their franchise. An elderly couple near retirement had to sell for personal reasons. It was my intent to better the lives of the franchisees, not to bear witness to such sadness.

It all changed in what seemed like one day—the bad luck, the feelings of bad timing came to an end; everything was different. What had happened? I went back to what I had said to myself while driving to the office. I had said, "Something good is going to happen to me today." I recalled an evangelist saying the same thing years ago: "Something good is going to happen to you today." I believe it wasn't just a positive affirmation, but somehow my determination to seek another way became the catalyst for change that I needed. I also kept repeating the words, "It won't always be this way" and it was all I needed to give me strength once again.

It was as if I was released from a prison. I was fifty-four years old and had spent twelve years building the franchise system. I didn't want to live the rest of my life in frustration. There had to be a better way.

> *"Something good is going to happen to me today."*

Things changed, and it appeared that all would be well. Driving to work was never the same after that day. The time it took me to get to the office became a pleasurable drive. I felt that twelve years of difficult times had come to an end. Each day became increasingly better.

I continued to tell myself every day that *something good is going to happen to me today*, and I haven't quit since.

Was it a coincidence, or was it an intervention? What had really happened that day? Weeks later, I found that my attitude had changed. I had renewed energy. I began to believe in my dream again. I really can't say what was going through my mind, but I was filled with true excitement. I wanted to buy out my partners and get my company back and own 100% of it.

Partnership Ends

After five plus years, my partnership with the Truck Outfitters and the other partners came to an end. Andrew Bilon's move back to Alberta had left me alone in B.C. to manage the company. It was during this time that I had a renewed interest. I felt it would also be the best time to buy out all the partners considering the share value was now at its lowest. Something inside me felt that the share value would increase under my renewed energy.

The last partner I bought out was Bill. By this time, he had seen that much of his money and investment diminish. I had professionals tell me that the value of his shares had declined greatly and that I should offer him cents on the dollar. Bill had given me $200,000 in good faith, a large sum in those days and I knew he had intrusted me with his money.

Bill continued as a silent partner for approximately 10 years. I must admit that the business plan I initially presented to Bill had its flaws. When I think back of that time it sounded typical of a young businessman's plan; *money will solve everything*. As I look back on it now it was a lesson learned, *money does not solve everything*.

Nevertheless, Bill was happy to be part of a new franchise organization. He volunteered to help in many occasions, cleaning, painting and store set-up. He had a great attitude and a willingness to work.

I remember visiting Bill and his wife at their home from time to time, giving them updates on the company, the financials and their investment. It was difficult for me to sum up the courage and make the regular visit. It was never good news, always a promise of better things to come that never happened. I remember arriving at their door and always being greeted with compassion, they knew that the visit wouldn't be good, but they always treated me with respect. It was a time when I had very little respect for myself, ashamed for not coming through on my promises and all the years Bill seeing us struggle.

It was their complete trust in me that led me to the decision to honor my word. I had no clue how I was going to do it, I didn't have the money, but I had my lawyer draft up an agreement that put it in writing, I would pay back Bill's entire initial investment for the few shares he had left. I didn't want him to lose a penny on the investment he made with me many years ago. I had always considered myself an honorable business man and I wanted to follow through with it. I think Bill and his wife were both shocked when Elaine and I presented them with the offer, a promise to pay back their initial investment. And as for me, I never felt so good in my life. I knew I had done the right thing. The agreement would give me ten years to pay the money back, but I managed to pay it back in just a few years.

And in addition we sold the two stores that I owned, Surrey and Langley to new franchise operators. The proceeds from the sale of the two stores, together with the inheritance I received from my Dad, gave me the money to buy out my partners. Could it be that I get to buy back the company I loved so much? Yes, it was true. I did buy back 100 percent of the shares in Cap-it, and it was one of the most exciting days I had experienced. I remember it well. A miracle! I couldn't believe that it could happen to me. This is another reason why I'm telling this story. I had to give up what I loved, just to get it back again. It was like a dream come true. I never imagined that someday I'd get my company back and own 100 percent of it. I was very happy.

Franchisees located in close proximity were also happy when I sold the two stores. Surrey was a very successful store; sales were higher than most other neighboring franchises when I ran it, and they felt that I may have been taking business from them. They encouraged me to get out of corporate store ownership, which happened to be the best thing for me. I'd use that money to build a better warehouse and buy out my partners. After 2003, we moved our warehouse to Gloucester Estates, an industrial centre for large warehousing to 175 Street, Langley, BC.

Strange thing about this move, the city of Surrey gave us an eviction notice at the warehouse location in Surrey because our fire sprinkler system did not meet their standards. They gave us one year to move. It was a rented building, and the landlord refused to help out. We had no choice but to move. As frustrated as we were, it ended up being a blessing in disguise. We were forced to move which gave us a better and bigger warehouse and office, closer to home.

The thought of owning 100% of the company filled us all with energy. Everything appeared to work this time. The move to Langley was the visual confirmation of a new corporate life we were all looking forward to. We found ourselves to be in the right place at the right time. Even things that we thought to be bad for us turned out for the best. The move to the new warehouse close to home in Langley was just the luck we needed. Timing couldn't have been better. Suppliers saw the move as a positive change and came to our aid with unbelievable support. The franchisees rallied behind us and gave us their full approval. Everyone enjoyed the new facility and especially now that it included head office with the warehouse. It was truly a new beginning for all of us.

2005: A Pivotal Point in Building a Better Franchise

Selling our two corporate retail stores (Surrey and Langley) and franchising them was the best thing we could have done at the time. It not only gave us the cash to reinvest in our new warehouse, but it allowed us to focus on the operational side of the franchise and supply them with product from our warehouse. For the first time in a long while, we were beginning to make a good profit at the head office and at the warehouse. We continued reinvesting through the years. We were able to spend millions of dollars on infrastructure, buildings, offices, education and training spaces, mock-up stores for training to warehouse equipment, machinery, picker trucks, forklifts, engineered seismic racking, computers, bar-coding, networks, programs, and equipment. Recruiting agencies were hired to help find the best most experienced people. People that had the extraordinary skill sets that could take us to the next level. People with experience in franchise law and sales, individuals with accounting expertise and financial analysis, marketing and branding skills, retail store designers, and architects.

We began with only four people in our head office, 27 years later, we had over 42 bright minds working on behalf of the franchise network. The final ingredient that brought our company to success was time and the many years of solving problems. Years of developing a great relationship with suppliers and manufactures. We developed a reputation for treating our sales reps with respect, inviting them to our franchise dinner cruises and our local trade shows. We now had the money and power to buy in container loads from China and truckloads from the USA. We could buy better and get preferred pricing. We had influence in our industry. Auto dealers were purchasing our franchise to operate alongside of their dealerships. Our brand became recognizable across the country through our marketing efforts. Beautiful stores were built.

16 Marketing

We started the franchise in 1990 with a royalty at 4.5%, the advice we were given by the professionals. Most royalties can run from 2.5% to as high as 9% in the franchise industry, with additional National Advertising Fund royalties, normally 2%, but can also be as high as 4%.

In 1993 we had been in the franchise business for only three years when we realized that our projected stores' profits were not where they should be. I knew something had to be done, and so I decided to reduce the royalty from 4.5% down to 2.5%, with 0% for national advertising. Most of the national advertising at that time was paid for out of my own pocket. We did everything we could to keep the stores strong in those years. There were times when special payment arrangements were made until their sales came up to a comfortable level. I even introduced a plan (integrated into the franchise agreement) that enabled new stores to begin with the low 1.5% royalty and slowly increase it.

A peculiar thing happened when we lowered the royalties. Lower royalties were introduced to increase the percentage of profits; but in many of the stores, it never did. We were interested to find that the franchisees just passed the savings on to their customers. We had to go back and explain the numbers to them to prove what was happening to their profits.

Our primary job as franchisors is to help franchisees at every level. They are not typical entrepreneurs, someone who can take risks and base success on their own talent. They buy into a proven franchise system so they can get the help and guidance to run a successful store. Helping stores understand the concepts we had learned was our responsibility. You must be a competent teacher to be a franchisor.

Today, all our stores pay a 3.5% royalty. We provide so much more support and education to the stores than in the early years. In those days, we had four people in head office; today we have 30 staff in head office, with 12 more in the warehouse, totaling 42 people to assist in running the head office.

We were always good at great store appearance, operations, and supply; but we were poor at training and ongoing education. We just didn't have enough people to do the job. We learned the hard way, and that it takes a small army of men and women to serve even seven stores.

I had invested in real estate in my private life, and it was this investment in real estate that I was able to finance to keep Cap-it alive during those early agonizing years. We solved one problem after another as quickly as we could, but it took almost seventeen years to finally reach peak performance.

***

Our growth appeared to be at a standstill in 2004. The two questions we asked ourselves were, How do we gain market share? And what can we do to keep momentum? Our new plan called for five stores to open per year. Up until now, we had opened an average of one to two stores per year, and some years there were none, and that was because infrastructure was still being put in place. In 2007, we awarded five franchises in one year—that was an awesome time. The question was, how do we keep that momentum? There were several things that contributed to this year of fast growth. First, we now had a better more impressive warehouse and corporate office. When applicants came to our facilities they saw a professionally run office and warehouse. Each staff member wore Cap-it logoed shirts. Cap-it logos where on most walls. Together with that they saw the storey board of the company's 40 year history clearly photographed and documented on a fifteen-foot wall, a mock up of a retail Cap-it store right off the board room and next to that a huge warehouse that carried over 60,000 part numbers. The warehouses' seismic racking towered above 27 feet high, with men lifted above by hydraulic picker trucks to pick product. Most applicants were more than impressed by the experience of the tour. Cap-it's corporate office and warehouse is impressive. Applicants get to see more than they expect. The real power of the franchise lies in the experience we give the applicants when touring our corporate facilities.

We began to think strategically and developed a ten-year plan. It called for us to continue opening stores throughout Canada, and if inquiries came in from the east, we would open stores as far east as Newfoundland.

We hired ahead, making sure we had talent in place for the expansion. We researched more warehouse space. Our focus was now on operations, never forgetting the stores and making sure they understood the figures and were able to make good decisions.

Now, how do we break loose and jump ahead of the competitors?

We knew that it wasn't going to be just one thing that would give us the boost we needed. I remember hearing from someone that infrastructure plays a major role in success. If you put the right infrastructure in place, your chances of success are tremendous. He went on to say that Las Vegas would not be the success it is if it didn't have several key elements of infrastructure in place. What were they? He continued to say that Vegas needed plenty of cheap electrical power, for their lights and air conditioners; and it just so happened that they are located near the giant Hoover Dam. Wow, that was lucky. Next, they needed water. They are located in the desert, but they have an endless supply of water from the underground aquifers and nearby Lake Mead. Next, they needed a local government that legalized gambling. Mix all this together with cheap desert land, and you have perfect conditions.

The question was, what were Cap-it's pillars of infrastructure? It was hard to tell, but I knew one thing, and that was that we just had to keep pushing forward and keep asking ourselves, *What do we wish for if money was no object?* Seventeen years had passed, and we knew we were still weak in marketing and operations.

A friend of mine told me, "Hank, it's never *one* thing." He meant the solution to a problem is never one single decision, and he was right. We found that we had to address all the issues all the time, and it eventually led us to what we wanted to achieve. Another businessman I know said, "To succeed, you have to get as many things right as possible." It was this approach that brought us to where we are today.

Adding more stores to our chain was our ultimate goal, but not at the expense of our existing franchisees. We decided that the new plan would begin with refining the operations of our stores. We knew that critical financial information was not getting through to the store operators, and something had to be done. If we could get the necessary financial information to the store operators, they could react to problems faster and make corrections before it became too late. We hired a financial analyst and a senior controller, both with the talent, experience, and skill set to deliver the appropriate information to the franchisees as well as to us. We also hired a specialized warehouse consulting team to study the efficiency of our warehouse and distribution centre.

We contacted many advertising agencies to advise us. The question we asked was, what can we do to appear larger than what we are, and what do you recommend that will take us to the next level? Should we hire a famous actor? Should we go on TV? What do you recommend?

It didn't matter who we spoke with; the answer always came back as *YOU DON'T HAVE ENOUGH MONEY.* TV is too expensive, your budget is too low, and the famous actor would be out of the question. Their recommendations usually came back as a flyer and radio campaign approach. One of the agencies even brought the head guy from one of the TV networks to announce that we couldn't afford TV. Go figure?

It was 1978 when I first saw this peculiar guy, Robert Schuller, a preacher, on television. Why I watched his TV program most

Sundays was hard to say. All I remember was that he preached a positive message, encouraging people, never condemning, and inspiring people to believe in their dream. I guess it was the dream thing that got my attention. Schuller had a dream, and I saw how it took shape through the years and became a reality. He started preaching from the rooftop of a drive-in theater and continued on to building one of the most beautiful glass cathedrals in the world, with millions of viewers watching his broadcasts. His story goes on to say that Billy Graham told him that it was television that took him to world notoriety in his ministry, and that Schuler, too, should try broadcasting. The rest is history. Robert Schuler became one of the most influential ministers in our time.

It was this memory that inspired me to see if there was a way we could possibly begin advertising on television. Eventually, we found the right agency and a man who knew exactly what we wanted to achieve. The amount we had to spend on TV advertising was not as important to him as the potential he saw in us. He had helped others to grow their companies, and he wanted to help us too. He showed us the awesome TV spots he had produced. The only issue that I can remember was whether or not to use the bull dog. The bulldog idea came from our advertising agent. He thought of hiring an actor dog, and felt that the bulldog breed represented the Cap-it brand best. He wanted the dog to say the word, "Cap-it" at the end of each commercial. Mentioning, that if a dog says it, it becomes more memorable. Go figure! You will see the bull dog leaning over the red Cap-it logo cube at the end of each commercial saying, "Cap-it" in a low voice. None of the executive team wanted the bull dog. But Jon, our media representative, convinced us that people identified with animals. He reminded us about the Aflac commercial with the duck and the gecko with the Australian British accent representing the Geico Insurance Company. Needless to say, the Cap-it dog was a hit. The first year of our commercials, we awarded five new franchises. The new momentum had begun. And better still, the franchisees loved it, especially when they found out that their faces would be included in the TV spots.

Jon's strategy was right; we would show the TV spots to the franchisees and present our plan. Jon had learned that if you filmed each franchise operator speaking on their own commercial there would be a better chance of them buying into the expensive program.

We analysed all advertising dollars that were spent locally by each store plus what corporate office spent annually on its National Advertising Program and combined it. It was a percentage of that figure that we used to come up with the amount that everyone was comfortable with. Each franchisee agreed to the increased monthly advertising royalty. We call it the (NAP) fund—National Advertising Program fund.

Next on the list was to improve our operations. Up until now, we had been working with an old computer software system at each store. Our warehouse and stores were not connected and could not communicate with each other. This was yet another piece of infrastructure we had to put in place. We eventually found a computer system in the USA that was used by a similar business that ran 1,000 locations. After many months of research, we decided that this software system would definitely have to be in place for us to grow. The problem was that the cost of the equipment and software was $750,000; and in addition to this, each store would have to pay $31,000 for their in-store hardware and software. It took us several years to pay it off, but it is now an essential piece of infrastructure we could not do without. The equipment takes up an entire room that must be air-conditioned, just to keep the space cool from the heat the equipment generates.

I remember presenting this to the franchisees. It wasn't easy asking them to come up with $31,000, plus pay a new monthly monitoring fee, when they thought that everything was working fine as it was.

Thank You

I must give a big-thank you to the franchisees that were with us during those early years of constant change. Not only through the introduction of our third computer change, but through the constant improvements we made to the system, and some of it costing each franchisee along the way. Reluctantly, they all agreed to implement the new equipment, and we offered financing to the stores that needed it. The new computer system combines a financial statement, inventory control linked up to the warehouse, and point of sale. And it doesn't end there. Our Business Intelligence Department could now study each and every sale providing necessary valuable information back to the store operators, keeping them profitable.

Our growth had its share of pain, and I remember the trip my wife and I took to visit each and every franchisee. The time had come, and I had to sit down with each owner and spend an evening at dinner explaining the hurdles we had to overcome at the head office and listening to their concerns and issues. Our many moves, our partnership troubles, and the constant changes got lost in communications with each other. Their concerns were not getting to me, and my concerns were not getting to them. And so we established a new system that would guarantee them direct access to myself and Andrew several times a year. Each sector in Canada would choose their representative annually to bring up issues and concerns and meet privately with Andrew and me. We call it the Franchise Owners Group. I believe the franchisees in the early years knew how hard we worked to improve the system; but we failed to emphasize the importance of good communications. The question we keep asking now is, "What keeps you up at night?" I especially appreciate the store operators who stayed with us for as many as fifteen and twenty years. And if you are one of those reading this, you know who you are. Thank you very much! I will always be eternally grateful for your support, the input and contribution you made in helping our franchise be the success it is today and helping to make this dream become a reality.

17   Cap-it Reaches the Summit

It's an awesome feeling to see where we are today, especially considering what it took to get to this point, with 30 locations. In 2012, we won the Canadian Franchise Association (CFA) Franchisee Choice Award. Our own franchisees selected us as great franchisors. We are in a period of real growth, and the momentum we so longed for is here. I'm well aware of what lies ahead and the work that is before us, so I'll keep on doing what I do best—motivating and encouraging others that their dream is possible. I know because all my dreams have come true. I am passing on my advice and experience to my sons, now managing the company, and to others in an effort to ease their way.

The one thing that needs mentioning is that Cap-it, through its evolution, has helped change the truck accessory industry as we know it. Cap-it's growth has shown competitors that there is profit in this business. When others saw Cap-it continuing to reinvest, they did the same. When they saw us build bigger stores, they did the same. When they saw us advertise on TV, they did the same. We came from a fragmented industry. In 1990, most of the industries' retail truck cap stores operated out of old service stations and on gravel lots. Today Cap-it is a world away; in many cases, we are in newly built upscale facilities operating in A locations, on main highways beside McDonald's and Wendy's franchises. Some auto dealerships are finding Cap-it a perfect fit for their dealerships.

Cap-it has been the first to sell products to the retailers (their franchisees) at low margins; others followed to compete. Cap-it was the first to introduce a large retail and wholesale color catalogue for customers to take home and read. They were the first to create retail flyers, advertise on TV, and build beautiful retail upscale stores with the greatest variety of accessories. Cap-it was the first to franchise the industry and build a chain of successful stores now spreading across Canada and the USA.

Whatever we do, we want to be the best at it. Like Ray Kroc (founder of McDonald's Restaurants) once said in the beginning, "We want to take the hamburger more serious than anyone else," and that has always been our motto. Cap-it is playing a major role in the shape of the new auto industry, and that's because we are taking the accessory business more seriously than anyone else.

Ever since 2008, when General Motors went broke and asked the US government for a financial bailout, much of the auto industry had to start over again; changes had to be made. They couldn't continue with their old style of doing business. Auto manufactures had to make a complete change in their thinking. They had to manufacture vehicles that people actually wanted to buy. And structure it so that their franchise dealers could make money. GM had also placed too many of their dealers too close to each other; nobody could make a profit. Dealerships were shut down to give way so others could survive.

According to the internet CNN News 2009/05/15

In May 15, 2009, General Motors notified 1,100 of its 6,000 dealerships Friday that it was terminating their ... Many are expected to leave the business this year.... Of the 900, about 500 will come from GM's plans to sell or close four brands.

We like to say, Cap-it is playing a role in shaping the new auto industry. Cap-it's role in this industry is in selling the adventure of the vehicle. This is something that auto dealers have never really tackled. Cap-it has proven that more money can be made selling the accessories for the vehicle than an auto dealer can make on the initial sale. Some auto malls have asked us to locate our stores inside the auto malls; they feel that Cap-it would be a good fit alongside the auto dealers.

Cap-it's tag lines, "Because Life's an Adventure," and "Genuine Truckware" speak to this philosophy. Look at the messages and images on people's T-shirts, their fancy stitched jeans, the paint jobs on their motorcycles, accessories and tattoos on the young people's bodies. We are in a generation of individuals who want to communicate a message. Same goes for their vehicles. They want their pickup trucks and SUVs to look different than their neighbor's, and they do this by accessorizing them.

Despite the personal desire to accessorize, there are also many customers that accessorize for business and industry, making the truck, van, and SUV even more useful.

Cap-it has positioned itself as a world class truck accessory store with strong brand recognition. Its goal is to keep customers for life. The latest addition to the accessory lineup has been the introduction of the tire department. Up until now, we only sold off-road tires and wheels; but now, with the introduction of the replacement tire program, we will be outfitting all cars and trucks with snow tires and replacement tires. Like we have often said, you can put all the accessories on a vehicle, but nothing looks as good as when you finish it off with a beautiful set of tires and wheels.

In addition, tires are an item that everyone needs, even in the lean years. We call it a must-have product, unlike a lot of our other products that we refer to as luxury.

Most of the products you see in our stores can be purchased elsewhere. What differentiates Cap-it is that we have brought together many accessory categories and placed them under one roof. We are a hitch shop, a tire and wheel centre, an off-road specialist, Thule racking centre, a truck canopy centre, and an accessory centre and an outfitter for the casual camper.

There are several things that separate us from the competitors and why we lead the industry. Our philosophy has always been sell yourself first, and the customer will buy from you. We do this through our branding. Everything we do at all points of contact must carry our message. "Because Life's an Adventure," "Genuine Truckware" speaks to our authenticity and our integrity.

Our brand communicates who we are: We are people who are earthy, love genuine things, value relationships; we have integrity, and we are at the leading edge of retail. Our stores are designed to impress the customer at the first step inside. If we don't get a wow at their first step, we have missed the mark. Our goal is to impress and overwhelm the customer by giving them a feeling that we are committed. We find that a beautiful, well-displayed store gives the customer confidence that they will be taken care of well. We want the customer to notice that we have spent time on the details, because that matters to Cap-it. Also, Cap-it will not advertise or display pictures or posters of any new truck. We let the auto dealers sell their own trucks; Cap-it wants to sell its own brand.

"Market yourself as average and that's all you will ever be," is another explanation of why we spend so much money designing and decorating our store showrooms and installation bays. I believe that the number one item a customer is looking for in retail, and maybe even in restaurants, is atmosphere. Second is product and service, and that would be the taste of food in restaurants. Atmosphere gives a customer an immediate feeling of commitment and confidence toward the store. They either like it or they don't. You get a good vibe or not.

"Market yourself as average and that's all you will ever be." The best way to explain what this means is to tell you a short story about a violin player. This violin player made over $1,000 an hour playing in the world's largest cities and concert halls.

> *"Market yourself as average and that's all you will ever be."*

One day he went to a very busy shopping centre in a busy city with his violin and began playing for people passing by. One lady recognized him and asked if he'd be there again tomorrow. Others stopped and listened; some just walked past. At the end of the day, the violin player collected $13 in tips. The moral of the story is *"Market yourself as average and that's all you will ever be."* You can have the most expensive item for sale, but if it's not displayed in accordance with the quality, it won't get the price.

The first sales counter we placed in our stores cost us approximately $350 to build. Today we spend up to $50,000 for a sales counter and back façade alone. Our multiscreen TVs can cost us as much as $30,000 each. Our first franchise turn-key package in 1990 sold for approx. $250,000. Today they sell for four to five times that amount. We spend tens of thousands of dollars on stores design and built-outs, all with a purpose of showing value and impressing the customer, and to make sure they get the Disney experience.

Getting connected: We call it getting connected. When you partner with the Cap-it group and become a franchisee, you are connected to

A successful team
Buying power
Technology
Marketing
Brand power
Training

Team: When you're connected to our team, there is no need to spend time hunting for the latest in truck accessories or trying to find the best-priced supplier, all of that is done by our team at head office. We want the franchisee to spend their time selling and serving customers. Getting supplier support and manufacturer co-op advertising is taken care of by the team. Conventions for franchisees are held two times a year, and there are additional franchisee owner group meetings.

Purchasing Power: Cap-it's distribution centre is state-of-the-art and covers approximately 75,000 square feet; it is located in Langley, BC, allowing for products to be shipped immediately to our stores. We maintain an inventory of over 65,000 part numbers, so there is no need to purchase in bulk to get the best price. Stores can purchase any item one at a time, and get best pricing from our warehouse. Cap-it bypasses the middleman. Bigger is definitely better when it comes to warehousing and Cap-it stores have the margins to prove it.

Technology: Technology means that stores are linked directly to the Cap-it warehouse order-and-distribution system in real time. The Cap-it system is designed to minimize the time needed to handle customers efficiently, confirm inventory, place orders, and, at the same time, capture marketing data, track sales, and make the back-office life of the Cap-it franchisee as efficient as possible

The stores are all linked by our special software, enabling them to order with a single keystroke. All financial information is tracked and monitored at the head office. Every detail is tracked and recorded, allowing the head office to supply valuable information to the store operator. Technology like this is important, because store managers can get carried away spending too much time working *in* the business instead of working *on* the business. We let the numbers do the talking, and our margins are there to prove it is useful.

Marketing: Cap-it franchisees enjoy the benefit of some of the most eye-catching advertising and marketing programs in the business. Our campaigns capture our exuberant style and speak directly to our target audience, consistently communicating the unique benefits of the distinctive Cap-it brand.

Our promotions—whether direct mail, in-store posters, or radio and television—are used to deliver strategic messages that focus on specific offerings. And our dedicated marketing department has the proven ability to deliver custom promotions into specific market areas in response to local and regional needs.

Training: We call it Cap-it College. Our training is one of the best in franchising. In the beginning, we gave the normal two-week training at head office and at a local store. Currently, we give six to eight weeks of training, and the training is done at the franchisee's store location. We found that the franchisee could only retain so much at one time, and if we wanted guaranteed success, we needed to put our team of instructors *inside* the franchisee's store and run it side-by-side with the franchise operator until they got it. Once the franchisee begins to operate their store, it is difficult to retrain them, so we thought we might as well start off doing it right the first time.

Training is focused on the presentation and adoption of a set of well-defined Best Practices, covering all aspects of the business. The very best in product and installation knowledge, combined with superior customer skills training, are the keys to sales development. Management training for inventory, merchandising and accounting, and staff development are the keys to profitability. This is accomplished with a custom-designed new store opening program combined with our ongoing in-the-field support by Cap-it operations personnel.

The Cap-it store is not like a pizza or a fast-food franchise (we refer to them as no-brainers). Our franchise requires many skills. Cap-it builds a beautiful store, gives the franchisee strong brand recognition, and supplies them with product at special pricing. The selling is up to the skill and ability of the franchisee.

18 Lessons I Have Learned from Failure

Far better it is to dare mighty things, to win glorious triumphs, even though checked by failure, than to rank with those poor spirits who neither enjoy much nor suffer much, because they live in the gray twilight that knows neither victory nor defeat.

—Theodore Roosevelt

NEVER EVER GIVE UP!

"Something worth having is worth waiting for." So easy to say and yet so hard to experience.

I have never gone broke or declared bankruptcy, and never even considered it. It was not an option. My mind-set was that I'd always pay my bills, and that I would succeed—if not now, then someday.

Failure, as much as it hurts, is an important part of life. In fact, failure is necessary. I'm not talking about small failures; I'm talking about the kind of failures that rock your world, completely altering the landscape of your relationships, finances, and mental well-being.

For those that have known true failure, and have bounced back from it, understand that failure is necessary for success.

The experience of failing at something is truly invaluable. Failure brings with it important firsthand knowledge. That knowledge can be harnessed in the future to overcome the very thing that inflicted so much pain in the first place. Nothing can replace the knowledge gained from failure

Failure builds character. You become proud of your accomplishments. You develop a deeper meaning and understanding about your life and why you're doing the things that you're doing.

It would have been nice if I had started my business with an MBA degree and had more business connections, but that's not what happened. Nevertheless, I learned not to be so proud that you fail to seek sound advice. If you're a know-it-all, you will surely fail. Learn to listen to others, hang around positive-minded friends, and walk away from the negative people. Believe in yourself and have faith.

I learned that few had a work ethic like mine, and not everyone had the desire to learn. I found out that few take responsibility for their own actions—it's always someone else's fault. And I found it difficult to help others when they don't need your help; they have all the answers even when things are going bad for them.

There are always answers to your questions. Look for them, read books, network and associate with like-minded people.

I have always had a desire to learn. I tell people I like to learn. Maybe it's this attribute that helps me take things a little farther than most and become the best at what I do.

And as I have said earlier in this book, be careful when fear comes to you. Fear unplugs you from thinking clearly. Fear destroys your creative thinking process. When fear comes, ask yourself, what's the worst thing that will happen to you? If you can live with that, your fear will leave you. Surrender and tell yourself it will always work out in the end. Don't mistake cautious thinking and planning as fear. Fear used to be my greatest enemy. Not anymore, because I believe something good is going to happen to me today. It's something that God gave me to believe in, in my darkest hour.

> *Don't mistake cautious thinking and planning as fear.*

Write down a pros and cons list, and you'll be surprised how you'll feel when it's all down on paper. It's not as bad as one thinks, and its one way of getting it out of your head and clearly looking at the problem.

Never franchise your business concept unless you have a great idea. A concept that others haven't thought of. Something that sets you apart from everyone else. Choose something that most people want and need. Then make sure you have a lot of money, an MBA degree, and a lots of business connections.

I began with little money, a grade 12 education, and the thought that my determination, faith, and skills at salesmanship would carry me to my goal. I was naïve. They say passion will always win over talent, but at what price?

It is easy to say that all you need are the three D's—drive, determination, and a dream. But in the end, you will risk your health, your family, your friends, and possibly your life—just to accomplish the future you dream of. There are always plenty of trade-offs and a price to pay. I guess that's what makes being young so beautiful; somehow you never weigh out the costs, you naïvely move forward.

The childhood fantasies that I embraced years ago exist in my life today. Memories are the anchor points of my life, where I find comfort. Much like tradition, it keeps me safe, and it gives me a connection to my past. I needed to be connected to the past because it gave me the sense of belonging. And it was this approach that kept my dream alive no matter how difficult the journey. Visions of sugar plums still dance in my mind; I continue to believe that my dream will become reality. The dream of many Cap-it stores across North America.

I experienced a lot in those first eighteen years, realizing the price that some people have to pay for their dreams. There seems to be a price on everything; nothing is free. Business laws are like all others in the world; obey them and they work, ignore them and they can destroy you. Good intentions are just that—they are not excused. Businesses survive by relying on and obeying business laws.

I needed a miracle. C. S. Lewis, in his book *Miracles*, debates with vigor the Creator's ability and privilege to interfere with his own laws. Some people think that they are special in their Creator's eyes, and rules will be broken for them. "God will take care of us, we don't have to plan for retirement, so we don't worry about tomorrow, because God will provide." But for the remaining 6 billion people on this earth, most have to live by the laws of the universe. Break one of them and you will suffer.

There are times that you can't do it alone; you can't solve the problem alone, and you need help. But you ask for it, and it doesn't appear to come. I will admit that I was one of those people. I know some people think that asking for help is a sign of weakness, but I never believed that. Today I still teach this principle in our Best Practices Book: *Please ask for help, it's not a sign of weakness but of strength.*

I needed some luck; I needed things to go my way for a change. I was responsible to many people, and they were counting on me to lead the company, to lead the franchisees into success. I needed a miracle.

> *Please ask for help, it's not a sign of weakness but of strength.*

It may sound discouraging, but if you've ever experienced some type of failure in your life, you probably brought it on yourself. I learned that if you're not happy with your circumstances, or where you are in your life, you're going to have to make a change. Remember, it is our philosophy that brings us to these places. You're going to have to change your philosophy. Our values, our traditions, and the things we hold sacred might have to be altered in an effort to bring us to the better place where we want to be.

It took me many years to realize that I was responsible for my own problems. Most of us tend to blame others. Originally, I blamed my parents and wished that they had taught me more business acumen so they could have helped me better. I blamed the industry I was in; I should have chosen an easier one like farming, protected by a marketing board. I will admit I blamed God as well.

It's easier when you can blame others. I have known friends and acquaintances who very seldom can point the finger of blame toward themselves; it's always others that are at fault. Some of you reading this right now are reminded of people you know that do this, but you think you're not one of them. Look at yourself honestly and ask, "Am

I one of them?" I was. Most people don't even realize that they are the problem too. They have been building this wall around themselves for so many years they can't see beyond it.

Einstein said it best: *"Insanity is doing the same thing over and over again and expecting different results."*

I spoke with this person some time ago regarding the difficult circumstances he was facing. He quite willingly pointed out that his current Member of Parliament was responsible for his dilemma. During an evening social, his MP had failed to recognize him, and to inquire how things were going. He was very distraught that his director had not come over to his table to see if there was anything that they could do to help him. In his

> *Einstein said it best: "Insanity is doing the same thing over and over again and expecting different results."*

mind, the problem lingered because his MP didn't care about him. By passing off the blame to the MP, he was adding yet another brick to the wall of protection around himself in an effort to stay blameless.

People hold others liable for a lot of things that happen to them. It's called *stonewalling*. After a while, stonewalling becomes part of your life, and you begin to enjoy it. It is always fun to blame someone else; it releases your pent-up anger. We build stone walls around ourselves so we're not at fault. Other people cause our failures. I finally realized I had to take responsibility for my own actions and force myself to take stock and reevaluate my beliefs before things would get better in my life.

I learned that I am the one to blame, and I must make the necessary changes to correct things. And as soon as you admit it, something wonderful happens. You are immediately filled with energy. Norman Vincent Peale calls this the *Power of One*. It only takes one person to change the world. And that's when I learned that *the weakest man's prayer is stronger than all the armies of the earth.*

My years of business very seldom allowed me the luxury to blame others, although I did struggle with it in the beginning. Have you ever had an experience in life where you changed directions and took a different route? If the route you chose forced you to turn back, you would have to go all the way back to where you initially went off track. I learned that a dead-end is just a good place to turn around.

Everyone goes into business for different reasons. For some its money and what they can attain; for some it is pride in ownership; and for some it is power. Even if you're unaware of your reason, time will reveal it in the end.

The business world is arguably one of the finest refineries of the human spirit and soul that one can experience. If you happen to still be in business by the time you retire, you have done well. Business will have taught you patience; it will have increased your knowledge, and it will have made you a better person. You will be as refined as gold by the time you finish. Not that I'm pure, but what fell away left me a better man.

19 Staying in the Number 1 Position

When we see industry change, the customer change, and the economy change, we have to react. Cap-it is all too familiar with adapting to a new environment. We've always survived by our creativity. Customers want help in understanding their needs, and it changes from one generation to the next. Today we are dealing with a generation called the Millennials (also known as Generation Y, Generation Me, and Echo Boomers) are the demographic cohorts following Generation X, born in the 1980s

It's a new generation that is asking for help in outfitting their weekends. They are hesitant to spend $1,000 on a sofa but will spend any amount on having a great weekend away at the lake or on a trail. Speaking further to the study of your customer, cereal companies have noticed a drop in cereal sales. And after many surveys and studies, they found out that the simple method of adding milk to the bowl of cereal was not working for this generation. They found out that this group of people didn't want to wash the bowl. They said it took too much time.

Our approach to fulfilling the needs of our customers this time was adding a camping division to our product lineup. We call it our adventure department. Funny thing is, it falls right into our trademarked motto, "Because Life's an Adventure." Our goal has always been to outfit a customer's vehicle for their adventure and in creating an adventure department we have been able to complete our goal. It helps bring in new customers who may not have come into the store and it helps to increase traffic.

Cap-it's strength has always been diversification. At the beginning, we began selling truck caps (toppers, camper shells), then we added truck accessories, hitches, then off-road suspension with tires and wheels; and recently, we added the adventure department. A department that falls right in line with our customer base, the casual camper. Their trucks and SUVs get outfitted with accessories for the weekend vacation and along with that, we sell all their camping needs. From inflatable boats, kayaks, fire pits, coolers, knives, grills, generators all the way to Go-Pro cameras and all at Best Prices! Cap-it's pricing is inline with all big-box stores. Being an upscale accessory store, we chose only the higher-quality adventure product.

The sheer number of our stores give us the buying power now, together with our flow-through distribution centre the ability to supply our stores with big-box purchasing power. What a great idea: Cap-it's small 4,000- to 8,000-square-feet store can compete with the giant 250,000-square-feet store. Our stores also work well in remote communities where there are few big-box stores such as Cabela's.

We had been studying the marketplace for years and asking ourselves, what product lines could we bring in that complements our truck accessory store, increase traffic, and increase monthly sales? Cabela's and Bass Pro Shop are public companies. They have shown that there is a real demand for their products. And in support of this, recent headlines in 2016 have said, "Retail Sporting Goods sales show that it's a $266 billion industry." Selling the great outdoors is a battle for the Casual Camper, and we want just a small portion of those sales. US sales of hunting equipment jumped 25% in the final quarter of 2012. The Canadian market is booming; sporting goods stores sold $4.9 billion last year, a 5% hike over 2012, according to Euromonitor. The 2012 Canadian Tire attributed an uptick in retail sales, in part to a renewed focus on the outdoors.

***

Even thought the US Automotive Aftermarket Industry is large at $38 billion, it doesn't even come close to retail sporting goods. Remember, sporting goods include running shoes; clothes, such as Lululemon products; sports equipment; camping equipment; and backpackers', golfers', hikers', and mountain climbers' equipment, and so on.

Cap-it has evolved and become a different kind of truck accessory store through this kind of thinking, and that's how we differ from our competition. We keep ahead of the retail curve.

Innovation

We have taken a page from Harley Davidson and other fine brands in America. You will see this in our latest store design in Dallas, Texas, and the new stores to come in Canada. Quite often, we'll find that some of our competitors have copied our store interior colors and features, but by the time it's copied, we have already moved on to another design. I feel lucky that I have been trained in artistic design and that I have always had a love for the arts. Art has played a big role in the life of Cap-it. It's always given us the creative juices that has kept our company ahead of the curve.

We have watched how Wolfgang Puck, world-famous chef, has taken fine dining to a new level and made it fun by bringing the kitchen right into the dining room. Patrons can watch their food being prepared while dining. Today it appears the norm in most restaurants, seeing the chefs prepare your food while you're dining, but there was a time that fine dining was separate from the kitchen. Wolfgang says, "I wanted to bring fun into fine dining." This concept was first brought into design by Wolfgang Puck in his first American restaurant in San Francisco. Along with his outstanding food creations and new recipes, his creative approach has helped catapult him to international stardom status.

Cap-it will also carry that theme in its new stores. We are bringing the service bays into the showroom. Customers will be able to watch vehicles being worked on through large plate glass windows while shopping. Another innovation first.

One of Cap-it's strengths has always been its ability to create. We like to say we survive because of our creativity. We are always looking out for our customer's needs, looking ahead and studying the marketplace and creating new experiences. We saw that our customers enjoyed the beautiful SEMA show in Las Vegas and how they displayed and presented truck accessories. SEMA (Speciality Equipment Market Association) We believe that the customer wants to see a retail store that has the professional Vegas look, and that is what Cap-it strives to do in their store design and layout.

Despite the many set-backs through the years we have always had the ability to read the marketplace and see in to the future. We forecast where the industry is going and how we can enhance the customers' experience. We research what new product our customer will want next season.

There's something that requires mentioning. All these innovations could not have happened if it were not for the great men & women that came along and joined us at head office. Each one added to the Cap-it System, improving it, making it easier for the franchisees to understand the System. Something we were always grateful for. Sean McGrath, our Senior Vice President was one of them. He brought the science of Data Mining to our company and created the Business Intelligence department. He is a talented man, he always said, "let the numbers do the talking" and they definitely did.

As per the Harvard Business Review, October 2016 Issue:

Data Mining has saved many large companies such as Popeyes chain of fast foods. In early 2000 the franchise was struggling–they had fired many CEOs.

They have 2,569 locations world wide (average franchisee had 7 stores) System wide sales 3.1B.

In 2007 they hired, a lady by the name of Cheryl Bachelder as CEO and it was her job to turn the company around. She has a great story. She says they were struggling for several reasons:

1. Lack of strategy
2. Too much short-term thinking
3. Very little consideration had been given to new-product innovation.
4. She says, "We had no arsenal of brand-building ideas".
5. She says, "We also had no national advertising, so consumer awareness was low"
6. Those problems, along with poor financial results, created an angry and frustrated group of franchisees.

The stock had dropped from $34 to $14 a share. What turned it around?

How do you turn a 3.1B company around?

Their first question was-Which group would be our top priority?

1. Stakeholders
2. Customers
3. Shareholders
4. Franchisees
5. Employees
6. Directors
7. Suppliers

The CFO argued for shareholders, and he had a point—the stock had dropped from $34 to $14. Then they discussed their customers. So, they tried legislating that restrooms had to be cleaned every 30 minutes and so on. And that went bad.

Here again, Finding solutions to the wrong problems–sound familiar?

The more her team talked about it, the more they saw the franchisees as their primary priority.

1. They have mortgaged their homes
2. Taken out large loans to open restaurants.
3. They have signed 20-year agreements.
4. No one has more skin in the game
5. They have no plan B.

> *Finding solutions to the wrong problems - sound familiar*

So, they asked themselves what can we do for the franchisees?

1. The franchisees said that their #1 concern was profitability
2. Next, they began focusing on the metrics that mattered most. How can we make them more profitable?
3. Next, they began with Data Mining for profitability (we call this Business Intelligence or Data Analysis) Data Mining was something they had never done.
4. They realized that Franchisees depend on profits for their income and for the cash flow to open new locations. They had never measured that number but began tracking it closely.
5. Next, they increased their National Advertising from 3% to 4% to create a bigger, better, stronger brand

So why am I telling you this story?

After 35 years of franchising, Popeyes had forgotten what their System was and what had made them a successful. Here's an example of a company that nearly failed because they didn't pay attention to Data Analysis / what we call-Business Intelligence.

Business Intelligence Department (Data Analysis)
Profit Is Job #1—Cap-it's Mantra.

Franchisees that follow the system do very well in attaining profits. Franchisees that don't follow the system pay the consequences. Business intelligence paves the way for store operators. They see a detailed list of key items that are critical to making a profit at month's end. The issue is, most business people fall into the trap of finding solutions to the wrong problems. That's where our business intelligence department comes in, to keep them focused on the real problems. It's so easy to forget that it's all about making a profit.

Knowing what to buy, how many to buy, and when to buy has become so important in today's fast-paced retail world. Trying everything possible not to get caught with dead inventory and making sure that you know how many to order in advance. This is where our Business Intelligence Department comes in. Although we have a million-dollar computer system, it isn't enough. You must have qualified operators who know what they are doing. We used to teach our stores to remember to work *on* their business and not get caught working *in* their business. Today, we have completely reversed that. We now instruct store operators to work in their business, while we at the head office will work *on* their business for them. We found that it was just too much for a store operator to keep track of all these things. Our daily business dashboard gives each store operator all the information needed to react quickly to any deficiency that may need immediate attention. There is daily communication with the franchisees and head office; each store operator must be aware and be able to react quickly to any deviation from the Cap-it success formula (the SYSTEM).

Items on the Dash Board

1. Traffic counts—the number of customers that walk through their store daily
2. Average ticket—the average sale of all products sold that day
3. Closing rate—the percentage of sales that are completed and sold that day
4. Gross profit—the gross percentage of profit made on the items sold that day
5. Labor sales—the percentage of labour sales compared to total sales that day
6. Category management—is extremely important when managing over 60,000 part numbers. Category management manages each department's sales and inventory, providing critical and accurate information in every category, line by line, item for item. Gives you knowledge of when to order, how many to order, what is popular and what is not.
7. Expense management—is analysed in the same way using category management and in addition creates a means (an average) of all stores and what the optimum expense should be in each category.
8. Inventory management—is analysed in the same way using category management. It gives the procurement department all the knowledge to make daily adjustments. It prevents having dead inventory and or ordering the wrong inventory. It also specifically points out the 80/20 rule, it shows that 80% of the sales are made with 20% of the products.

We like to say that we have taken a complicated industry that has over 2 million part numbers and made it simple for someone to operate. We have narrowed it down to just over 60,000 part numbers. We have a set of Best Practices in place that teach our operators how to run a business, make money, and serve customers. And we don't believe in next-day service like most of our competitors. We strive hard to give the customer same-day service by having the popular items in stock. We know that our competitors can get anything the next day, but at Cap-it, they can have it the same day. We have a very sophisticated computer system and programmers that do all the work for you. It's called category management.

Surrounding Yourself with the Best

We've instituted the Jack Welch Session "C" employee evaluation system. Welch is the former CEO of one Americas largest companies, General Electric. After years and years of trying to find out which employee is performing, which one should get a raise in pay, which one needs to go, and which one should you hire, Jack Welch helped simplify it.

The top two traits one should look for during the interview process:

1. Does this person exude energy?
2. Do they have the ability to energize others?

Skills and education go without saying.
Top items to evaluate during the employee review:

What is their "buy-in" level to the company? (graded on a scale from 1 to 8)
What is their "skill level"? (graded on a scale from 1 to 8)

And in addition, the following employee traits need to be rated:

Rate as Needs improvement, Satisfactory, or Excellent
Customer focus—Customer is the highest priority.
Energy—Full of energy.

Energize—Energizes others.

Creative—Always comes up with new and bright ideas / bettering the company.

Executes—Completes the task and does what he says.

E-business = Awesome in computers, technology, systems, and procedures.

Cap-it system—Knows and follows the system.

Each employee is asked to rate themselves. Then the supervisor is asked to rate the employee. After this, the supervisor can have a real discussion on the differences. The final goal here is to see how the employees see themselves according to your assessment. The next step is to find the people in the organization that are in "the Top 20%." These are your best top performers that need to be recognized and rewarded accordingly. Who are in the Vital 70%? These are the people that can be promoted to the Top 20%; however, some may desire to stay in the Vital 70%. Not all want to be in the Top 20%; some are content, but are still vital to the company. The final task is to find who are in the Bottom 10%. These are the ones that need to be replaced because they don't contribute anything vital to the company.

Entering the USA

Opening stores in a new community, in another country that has never heard of Cap-it isn't easy. The three years of research and planning however did pay off despite the many times we felt like giving up. The average home in Texas sells for less than half of what they do in Canada, but the rents of commercial property are exceptionally higher, much higher than in Canada. Each time we came across a great location, the rents were so unreasonable we had to walk away. It became very frustrating. Local real estate agencies are not like they are in Canada. MLS in Canada stands for a Multiple Listing Services, something they don't offer in Texas. Realty offices in Texas don't offer

MLS services making it very difficult to see what is available through-out the county. Each realty office is on their own, another stumbling block in finding suitable locations.

In 2017 we set up a great looking franchise sales booth at the SEMA show in Las Vegas. We were very surprised at the response, we didn't know what to expect or how we would be received. However, word had gotten out in our industry that Cap-it was opening stores in conjunction with Leer. The reception of a Canadian company coming to America and opening stores was well received. Hundreds of curious business people stopped by the booth asking us about the Cap-it system and to our surprize many people asked us about the merits of converting their current store to a Cap-it as an exit strategy.

SEMA with its annual attendance of over 70,000 domestic and international buyers was an excellent place to debut and market our franchise.

After 3 years of researching the Dallas, Fort Worth area we finally found a beautiful site in Haltom City with a reasonable lease rate. Its located on the busy Denton Highway. The decision was made that our first store would be run and operated by ourselves corporately to showcase Cap-it's latest store design to the DFW community.

Our new store design is like no other in the industry. Atmosphere is paramount and is one of the strategies Cap-it uses to show custom-ers how serious we take the truck accessory industry.

During those three years of research and planning we have met many wonderful people. Influential people that have encouraged us in our efforts. In addition to the opening of our first store, others in the industry have shown interest and asked to convert their truck accessory store to Cap-it. We are hoping that this is the beginning of great things to come.

We found that the retail light truck accessory industry is frag-mented and unorganized. Cap-it appears to have an answer that is fast becoming attractive to many people in the USA. We are taking a complicated industry and making it easy for new people to operate.

The American market is so much greater than the Canadian market and it looks like Cap-its future could be in the USA. Like I have said earlier, my dream always included entering the USA market. Twenty-eight years ago, I named our company, Cap-it International with the absolute intention of expanding internationally into the USA. Its just taken a while for this to happen but is now given me much joy seeing it come together.

The power of the DFW Metroplex

The population of the Dallas–Fort Worth Metroplex is 7,399,662 according to the 2017 US Census, making it the largest metropolitan area in Texas, the largest in the south, the fourth-largest in the United States, and the seventh-largest in America. DFW ascended to the number one spot in the nation in year-over-year population growth. In 2016, the metropolitan economy surpassed Houston, to become the fourth largest in the U.S with a 2016 real GDP just over $511 billion. As such, the metropolitan area's economy is ranked 17th largest in the world. As of January 2017, the metropolitan job count has increased to 7,558,200 jobs.

If one added up the population in all our 30 stores territories in Canada, it might not even come close to the population in the DFW metroplex.

LA Times reported, Toyota's U.S. sales chief, Bill Fay, said consumers' shift from cars to SUVs is one of the most dramatic the industry has ever seen. 2013, Trucks and SUVs represented 50% of the U.S. market. They closed 2016 at 63% of total sales, and analysts don't see that changing anytime soon. The Shift from Cars to Trucks and SUV's has happened. Jacqueline Hansen states in her 2018 CBC news report that trucks and SUV's now represent 68.2% of all vehicles in Canada. This is all good news for Cap-it stores! 2018 Ford announced that by 2022 the only car they will produce will be the Ford Mustang. All their attention will be on building Trucks, SUV's & Vans.

Boomers and millennials both like the space and the higher ride that SUVs offer, and improvements in fuel economy make them competitive with cars.

2014 Autos Writers, Terry Box, of the Dallas News, says Texas may be the center of the pickup-truck universe. In pure numbers, Texas still dwarfs everyone else, with 322,000 pickups sold in the Lone Star State last year, and that's not counting the all the SUV sales.

In 2015, we were asked if we would be interested in opening stores in Dallas and Fort Worth, Texas. Our supplier of truck caps, LEER, TAG (the Truck Accessory Group) in America wanted to have dealer representation in that area. They told us that it is one of America's most populated cities, with some of the highest percentages of truck ownerships in America. A population of approximately 7 million just in the Dallas and Fort Worth communities.

We were asked much the same question back in 1993, with disappointing results. Why now? This time they said that they didn't want to own the stores; they wanted us to own the stores, with the condition that we sell their product exclusively. LEER went on to say that they didn't have proper representation in that city for the past twenty years and that we came highly recommended.

After a year or more of negotiations, we finally came to an agreement on a working relationship. Contracts were drawn up and agreed upon.

Cap-it is not well known in the USA; however, LEER has a great following and a recognizable name with an excellent reputation for quality. We didn't want to go though all the pain we had in developing our name back in 1990 in Canada. It could take a long time in developing Cap-it in the USA. That didn't appeal to me. We thought cobranding with LEER would give us the shortcut so the agreement is for the Dallas and Fort Worth areas.

At this point, we have set up our US offices in, Irving, Texas. Our offices are located on the top floor of a high rise in Las Colinas. I made sure that I could see JR Ewing's office tower from my window. Reminds me of the TV show *Dallas* and JR Ewing. I loved to watch that show. How exciting and funny at the same time! I never dreamt we'd be doing business in Dallas, go figure. I thought that this part of my dream was dead in 1993. So, here we are in the early stages of opening franchise locations in DFW.

We have passed our US Franchise Disclosures, spent the money on research and development, traveled around to every possible competitor, put on hundreds and hundreds of miles. We are doing our due diligence in an effort to prevent any surprise. What I can tell you is that the Texas people are wonderful. You could say redneck, but a little different from Alberta. They are very faith oriented. They have many churches there. Locals refer to it as the buckle of the Bible Belt. It's not uncommon to have one hundred people or more in a church choir. Church attendance can average 3,000 to as high as 26,000. TV evangelist Joel Olsten has a very large church in Houston.

The AT&T Stadium can hold 100,000 people and is fifteen stories below ground level. There are huge freeways, continually being upgraded and improved because of the constant influx of people and companies moving in. Funny thing, from my personal survey the average home sells for less than half of the home prices in the greater Vancouver area.

Since 1990, at the beginning, Cap-it has had its marks registered and trademarked in all 50 states, knowing from the onset that the US market was where we wanted to grow. Most of what we sell in Canada comes from America; of course, it makes sense for us to expand into the USA. It's a much bigger market. America's population is ten times that of Canada. According to our population per Canadian store numbers, we could open eighteen stores in the Dallas and Fort Worth area alone.

The market is changing. There's so much competition; customers are more informed that ever before. Amazon's online sales, manufacturers are selling direct to the consumer, big-box stores and Costco all fighting to keep up revenues. Manufactures are linking up with strong retailers like ourselves, where you can order it online and pick it up at one of our many locations. And Cap-it, with its upscale retail approach, can easily compete with the big-box retailers because of its huge buying power. Cap-it uses much the same internal flow-through systems as Home Depot.

Our strategy for setting up stores in DFW is much the same we use in Canada. We approach the market in four areas.

- First, we are very interested converting existing truck accessory businesses to our brand. We have done this many time before and it works very well.
- Secondly, we are interested in, buying out existing truck caps dealers. Dealers that may want to retire or exit the business, it's a great exit strategy for some.
- Thirdly we seek for new ground in which we can construct our own building.
- And fourth we seek for locations and building that we can renovate to suit our needs.

The interesting thing about the Cap-it franchise is that it's not a pizza franchise or a restaurant, where you have to put in sixteen to eighteen hours a day. We are open eight hours a day, and you get Sundays off. You're not stuck behind a kitchen. Here you can talk to customers, visit local auto dealerships, install accessories, and even drive the forklift. It's a fun business, unlike a transmission shop where buying a transmission can be a grudge sale. Our customers are always happy when making a purchase. It's a fun business where you can raise your whole family. Many franchisees have been with us for well over fifteen years. We have low turnover rate.

27
Years Later

You are searching for the magic key that will unlock the door to the source of power; and yet you have the key in your own hands, and you may make use of it the moment you learn to control your thoughts.

—Napoleon Hill

Another Time

However, the one thing that I always taught my franchise operators had now affected me. I had always taught them that when you buy a Cap-it franchise, your life will change—and it should be for the best. In my opinion, you can't build a great company and not become a great person. I believe that most millionaires can become wonderful people. You don't find too many wealthy people who are jerks.

I had changed, and what I had noticed the most was my attitude. The years of anguish and disappointment had left their marks on me. I had become resentful, bitter, jaded, and even lost my confidence. I was sabotaging my own dreams at a point, because I didn't really think I deserved to succeed. Have you heard the term *stinking thinking*? I'm not certain if I had that disease, but I can tell you, if you're not plugged into some positive principles, one can develop a *stinking thinking* attitude very quickly. The day that I began to affirm that "something good is going to happen to me today," my attitude was changed. Something inside me said I deserved better. I had spoken those words in what was probably my darkest hour.

It continued to build; day by day I could see the difference in myself. Up until now, fear had played the biggest role in my personal defeat. I learned that when you're fearful, you can't think, you can't plan, and you can't create. You're no good to yourself or your company. You need to find a source that will feed your mind with positive philosophy, and you need to forgive yourself.

I started to spend more time with new friends, positive-minded people. I began to read new books and continued to recite positive affirmations to myself. I noticed that what I said had dramatic effect on others besides me. Reciting positive affirmations brought me new life. The most important thing is to be in the right place at the right time, and I believe that's something we often can't control. I learned if you ask God, He will help you do that. I also learned that fear, envy, bitterness, and lust will rob us of what we deserve. I didn't want to be the tail anymore; I wanted to be the head. I wanted to get my confidence back, and I wanted my dream to come true.

Looking back, I can see that my partners had taught me many things. There were times I wished for help, an uncle of sorts, like Lee Iacocca, former president of Chrysler, who could give some direction, or even Jimmy Pattison, a business magnate, who began by selling cars in Vancouver BC to becoming a billionaire, a local hero. And in some ways, I did get my wish. My partners, in fact, did show me the other side of business that I wasn't aware of. They were good at operations. Together we became a team. I recognized them for their talent. In the end, though, the partnership was dissolved. They got most of their stores in Alberta redecorated, looking much more professional than they did previously, and I got to duplicate their warehouse in BC. Western Warehouse which is now an integral part of the supply chain to the Cap-it franchisees.

Now I am a chairman and CEO of a large company, but my goal of bettering the lives of others had nearly destroyed me. I see that all those dark and difficult years had a purpose, and I believe that I paid the price. Sometimes I ask myself why the company didn't fail. It should have failed many times according to our balance sheet; and all I can say is that after losing almost everything, financially and psychologically, I kept one thing, and that was my belief and my faith that someday it would work out.

A funny thing about clichés—such as *to succeed you have to get as many things right as possible* and *it's never one thing, everything matters*—many professional speakers impress you with words like these, and they are not wrong. They are great words to live by. But saying words and putting them into action are completely different things. I believe you can be judged by what you say, but even more judged by what you achieve.

Interestingly enough, I guess that success too early in life can breed arrogance. When you are arrogant, you think you know it all. And when you know it all, you can't learn anything new.

Even though I am the chairman and CEO of the company, my sons Mason and Andrew now run and manage it, together with some very bright and talented people. Elaine and I are still involved in the big decisions. My sons have a passion that rivals mine. They are very smart, well-educated, and experienced young men whom I love to work alongside. It's a family business; my wife, Elaine, both of our daughters-in-law, Brenda and Kim, play an integral part of the management team; we enjoy the truck accessory industry, and we have always enjoyed each other. They are as excited as I am about taking Cap-it into the future. Mason and Andrew both understand the complexities and the creative nature that one must possess to build a great organization.

I have wondered many times why I decided to franchise my business. Was it for the money or for something else? I think if it had been for the money I would have chosen an easier route.

I was building something the world had never seen; they said it would never work—and that must have challenged me. It was up to me to get people to buy into the vision. Selling them on the big picture was relatively easy; however, keeping it successful was another thing. In addition, so much of the business depended on the franchisee's skill set and their business abilities. Selecting the right candidate took energy and discernment. I found that not everyone had the desire to learn.

I had to adapt quickly and change my strategy on the fly about teaching and educating people on the basics of running a business. Instead of building the business, I spent most of my time learning how to teach others.

All I can say is that something inside me must have known that educating people would be a big part of my life. Because although I do enjoy it, I just never knew how difficult it can be when someone comes to class who really doesn't want to learn. I have a friend who said that she loves to learn. I was taken by surprise by that statement. I thought about it and realized I too was a person who loved to learn. To be a franchisor, you must be a good teacher and a franchisee must have a desire to learn. If you are one that does not love to learn, chances are your business will show it.

The dream I had of building this franchise extracted a high price. Why did it take so many years to perfect the business? Why did I personally experience so many years of bad luck and bad timing? Why were the struggles so intense? Why had my dream nearly destroyed me? Was I a problem-solver who was so intent on solving problems that I ended up creating problems just so I could solve them? Did I feel that I didn't deserve my dream? Or did I sabotage my own dream? So many questions with so few answers.

It's taken me quite some time to write this book and a few additional years to conclude it. I am hoping that my frankness and willingness to reveal my own weaknesses may give readers a better understanding of the price that they too may be asked to pay. Upon reflection, I realized that I had to delete some of the content I had included. Mainly complaints about the unfairness of it all and the anger of going through years of struggles. However, I wanted to pass on to others what I had experienced; maybe someone can learn from it, or it may be of assistance to others who are going down this road. Or just to let them know that I was one who passed this way, too. I wanted to give my struggles some meaning and purpose, if only to show others the price that was extracted, and the trade-off, and that I did receive a reward.

THE PRICE OF MY DREAM

There have been many times that I felt that my business life ran parallel to the ancient story of Joseph. Joseph was thrown into a well by his brothers and given up for dead because of jealously. He was then rescued by passing merchants and sold into slavery. Joseph was then sold to a high-ranking Egyptian named Potiphar and eventually became the supervisor of Potiphar's household. He excelled at his duties, became one of Potiphar's most trusted servants, and was put in charge of his household. After being falsely accused he was sentenced to prison for a period. During his time in prison he developed a reputation for being wise and helpful, so much so that the king called for his advice. For his advice and wisdom, he was given the position of ruler over all Egypt, only second to the king.

Joseph was in-charge of storing up food during the years of plenty and selling it to Egyptians and foreigners during the years of famine. During these years of famine Joseph's brothers came to buy grain from Egypt and met their lost supposedly dead brother Joseph. Too their surprize Joseph forgave his brothers because of their repentive attitude for what they had done.

There were many distressing circumstances I found myself in, and some of them may have been unjust, as were those in Joseph's life. However, as I learned from the account of Joseph's life, by remaining strong and faithful, we can be confident we will be rewarded in the fullness of time. Who would blame Joseph if he had turned his brothers away in their need?

Joseph's story also presents amazing insight into how to overcome obstacles and difficulties. After all his ordeals, Joseph was able to persevere, believe in himself and keep the faith.

The things I had learned after years of wondering why finally began to make sense, and I eventually caught on to what was happening. I'm proud that I was one of the men that successfully used what was given to me. The uncertainties I faced in my life changed my values. I believe the ideas, thoughts, and attitudes I had that fell away left me a better person. What transformed me was a healthier attitude: serving without recognition. The adversities and the uncertainties served to bring me closer to the better place. Uncertainties became my friends, and I looked forward to implementing their outcomes.

One of the pieces of literature that has meant much to me was the poem Invictus. It's been quoted by many people from Winston Churchill to Nelson Mandela to U.S. prisoners of war in Vietnam. It has lent its title to a movie starring Morgan Freeman and Matt Damon. It is often quoted in troubled times for its triumphant tone and uplifting message.

Invictus

Out of the night that covers me,
Black as the pit from pole to pole,
I thank whatever gods may be
For my unconquerable soul.

In the fell clutch of circumstance
I have not winced nor cried aloud.
Under the bludgeoning of change
My head is bloody, but unbowed.

Beyond this place of wrath and tears
Looms but the Horror of the shade,
And yet the menace of the years
Finds, and shall find me, unafraid.

It matters not how strait the gate,
How charged with punishments the scroll,
I am the master of my fate:
I am the captain of my soul.

William Ernest Henley
(1849-1903)

It was written in 1875 and published in 1888, without a title. The title was added by Arthur Quiller-Couch, editor of *The Oxford Book of English Verse* (1902).

I feel that somewhere inside each of us there exists a spirit that wants to conquer and defeat the darkness that plagues us all. I'm glad that I chose to believe in things unseen—because I've known them to become a reality.

I have learned that you have the power, to call upon those things that don't exist, and they will.

1977 The Early Years
Rover Recreation Centre

1977

- We sold RV supplies and manufactured Truck Canopies. At our highest we carried over 350 truck canopies in stock. Our small manufacturing facility allowed us to build 8 canopies per day per man.

1979

- The introduction of Sundance Trampolines and Camping Equipment
- Awarded the Highest Canadian Sales Award for Sundance Tampolines

1980

- By now we wanted to become a true retailer of recreation. We continued this by introducing new products such as Spas & Pool Supplies and National Billiard Tables.
- Awarded the Highest Canadian Sales award for National Billiard Tables.

Abbotsford Store 1979

Sons Mason and Andrew now running company.

1980 The Ultra-light Days
Eagle Ultra-Lights

1980
Very exciting times!

We became an authorized flight instruction facility for Eagle Ultra-lights based out of New Mexico. Hank sold and gave flight instruction to well over 65 customers. Although flying was his passion for many years the company had to sell the division for liability reasons.

Rover was one of the most exciting stores in Abbotsford at the time. There never was a store quite like Rover, customers would walk in and be over whelmed at the variety of recreational products. They would see Swimming pools, Spas, Kayaks, Billiard tables, Ultra-light aircraft, Pin ball machines, Camping equipment, Truck Canopies and more.

Above Photo: Taken in Albuquerque New Mexico at Bert Ruttan's airfield during Hank's official flight instruction schooling. Hank is in the American-Eagle prototype called the Falcon. • Cruising speed of 100mph • Enclosed cockpit - a first in its day • Canard wing. The American Eagle Ultra-light people were, Brian Allen - the first person to peddle power an aircraft across the English Channel and Larry Newman the first person to air balloon across the globe in the Albatross II.

Hank at 1000 feet

Rover Recreation retail store.

1985
Poolmart & Dufferin

The Poolmart & Dufferin days

1985 - The recession of 1982 marked an end of an era. We now had to compete with the discounters and big box retailers, so we split up the, "have it all under one roof philosophy" into three separate stores, Poolmart, Dufferin and Rover.

As a result Poolmart became our speciality swimming pool and chemical store, opening it's doors just 1/2 mile down the street in Abbotsford on South Fraser Way.

The Dufferin Game Room store franchise replaced our billiard department, and as well opened next to Poolmart. Despite great sales and profit the decision to sell was made.

After the sale of both Poolmart and Dufferin, Hank moved the truck canopy store to a larger facility across the street and opened his second Rover location in Surrey in 1988.

Dufferin's Game Room Store - Hank and Elaine with Dufferin's Director of Operations, Larry Schbourack of Toronto.

Opening week of BC's first Dufferin Game Room Store Franchise:

1990
1990 End of Rover
Start of Cap-it

1990 – The Birth of Cap-it®

In an effort to franchise we had to change our name. Land Rover of England prohibited us from franchising our concept under the Rover name.

Rover held the world copyrights to any and all automotive products. The difficult task of selecting a name now began, we finally settled on the catchy name Cap-it; the original idea came from the thought - if you own a truck – we can Cap-it. Hence Cap-it Canopies.

The opening of Cap-it franchise's began immediately.

Richmond store - as you can see on the re-o-graph sign we sold truck canopies for as little as $399.00. At this time canopies came in colored gel coat only. (17 different gel colours) Painting and colour matching had not yet been established.

Hank speaking to the new franchisees at the Semi-ah-moo Hotel and Resort in Washington.

Photo taken at the Abbotsford location in 1990. You can see the old Rover logo sign set to the side and the new Cap-it Canopies illuminated sign newly installed.:

2007 – 30th Anniversary

2007 marked our 30th year in business. The milestone was significant and a great accomplishment considering that we were the first people to develop a successful franchise concept in the truck cap industry.

In 2003 Hank again invested more time and money in the company he founded and in 2003 bought out his last major partner. His passion for elevating the simple truck cap store to a new level remained and in 2006 introduced many new initiatives that would further his dream.

2005 - the opening of our Coquitlam store – Coquitlam incorporated all of our newest interior designs, Branding and marketing techniques and became an instant success.

2006 was a year of significant changes.

- Professional franchising staff came on board
- Our name changed from Cap-it The Truck Outfitters to Cap-it Genuine Truckware™
- "Because life's and Adventure" became our new motto.
- The Cap-it logo was changed from the eclipse to the red square.
- The introduction of Branding created a whole new look and set a new standard in the world of truck accessories.
- A new store interior was developed and created by several leading Canadian design groups.
- The new concept exterior store was designed and created by Harold Funk Architects in Manitoba.
- The opening of our new education facility and training store.
- The opening of our new warehouse and corporate offices on 275th street.

Coquitlam store was the first to adopt our new branding and image

Abbotsford was our first store – opened October 7th, 1977

2017-18
US Expansion

AMERICA'S TRUCK ACCESSORY STORES™

NOW IN TEXAS!

DALLAS / FORT WORTH

30 LOCATIONS IN CANADA & USA

New Franchise Opportunities now available!

TIRES • RACKING • OFF ROAD • HITCHES

NOW OPEN! IN HALTOM CITY, TEXAS

5837 Denton Hwy.
Haltom City, Fort Worth

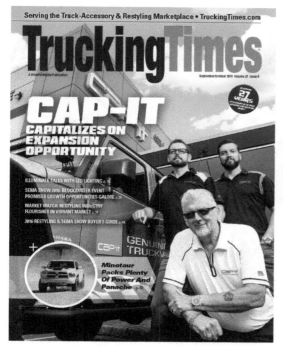

Industry recognition, and
2017 SEMA Show booth
with franchisees.

2018

2018
Expansion into the USA brings about new store upgrades and design. Items such as graffiti walls, flooring, sales counters, multi-screen TV's, signage and large glass shop walls are introduced.
Joint venture with LEER gives birth to a new name in the USA, Cap-it Americas Truck Accessory Stores, in Dallas, Fort Worth Tx.

2017 SEMA Show Las Vegas, Nevada

Hank with sons Mason and Andrew.

Elaine Funk with daughter-in-laws Kim and Brenda Funk.

International Corporate Office
Langley, Canada

USA Corporate Office
Irving, Texas

Painting in my Art Studio

2001 Ellensburg Rodeo Poster

About the Author

Hank Funk grew up in Abbotsford, BC. At the young age of nineteen he had started his own successful sign painting business. And at the age of twenty two he became top salesman of the year selling carpets in 1973, and in 1977, he started his first truck accessory store. He would grow the business to 30 locations and become the largest chain of franchise truck accessory stores in Canada and the USA.

He is the founder and CEO of Cap-it International Inc., married to wife Elaine, and they have two sons, Mason and Andrew, who work in the company as president and vice president

He has forty years of experience in the retail industry; twenty-eight of those years have been spent developing and operating the Cap-it Genuine Truckware franchise concept.

Hank's first love has always been art, but with a talent for business, he has been nominated for Entrepreneur of the Year and received Franchise Choice Award from the Canadian Franchise Association. He has won many awards in Canada and the USA for his artistic skills. He studied Artistic Design at Vancouver's School of Art. Completing his studies of Christian philosophy, he developed a talent as and educator and a love for helping people fulfill their dreams.

He is a member of the Federation of Canadian Artist (FCA), International and Canadian Franchise Association, IFA, CFA, LTAA, and SEMA.

CPSIA information can be obtained
at www.ICGtesting.com
Printed in the USA
LVHW020536080519
617021LV00007B/12/P

9 781641 146241